S. Hrg. 113–286

SUCCESSES AND CHALLENGES OF MEETING SUSTAINABILITY GOALS IN HAWAII AND THE PACIFIC

HEARING

BEFORE THE

SUBCOMMITTEE ON WATER AND POWER

OF THE

COMMITTEE ON ENERGY AND NATURAL RESOURCES UNITED STATES SENATE

ONE HUNDRED THIRTEENTH CONGRESS

SECOND SESSION

TO

EXAMINE THE SUCCESSES AND CHALLENGES OF MEETING SUSTAINABILITY GOALS IN HAWAII AND THE PACIFIC, INCLUDING OVERSIGHT OF EXISTING ACTIVITIES AND FEDERA-ISLAND PARTNERSHIPS IN ENERGY, WATER, LAND USE, MARINE RESOURCES, AND OTHER SECTORS

HONOLULU, HI, APRIL 16, 2014

Printed for the use of the
Committee on Energy and Natural Resources

U.S. GOVERNMENT PRINTING OFFICE

88–082 PDF   WASHINGTON : 2014

CONTENTS

STATEMENTS

SUCCESSES AND CHALLENGES OF MEETING SUSTAINABILITY GOALS IN HAWAII AND THE PACIFIC

WEDNESDAY, APRIL 16, 2014

U.S. SENATE,
SUBCOMMITTEE ON WATER AND POWER,
COMMITTEE ON ENERGY AND NATURAL RESOURCES,
Honolulu, HI.

The subcommittee met, pursuant to notice, at 1:10 p.m. at the East-West Center at the University of Hawaii, Manoa Campus, Honolulu, Hawaii, Hon. Brian Schatz, presiding.

OPENING STATEMENT OF HON. BRIAN SCHATZ, U.S. SENATOR FROM HAWAII

Senator SCHATZ. Good afternoon—the Subcommittee on Water and Power is holding a field hearing here in Honolulu. We're pleased to have all of you.

We are here today to examine the successes and challenges of meeting sustainability goals in Hawaii and the Pacific. Hawaii is a national leader in sustainability and we want to continue to encourage that strong tradition. We'll discuss existing Federal-Island partnerships in energy, water, land use, marine resources and other sectors as well as initiatives by local and State government.

This weekend the United Nations International Panel on Climate Change released a stark report on the need for all countries to begin reducing carbon pollution immediately in order to avoid the most devastating impacts of climate change. Following its release Secretary of State, John Kerry, said this report makes very clear we face an issue of global willpower not capacity. Secretary Kerry is correct. We have the tools necessary to win this fight. What we need is the will, at all levels, to use them.

Hawaii is one example that the statement is making progress. But it is also a place that will suffer if climate change continues unchecked. Hawaii's geographic isolation, limited physical resources, unique ecosystems and growing population create a unique set of challenges.

We need reliable and affordable energy, water, agricultural land and other resources that are vital to a sustainable and growing economy. U.S. affiliated Pacific Island territories and freely associated States face similar challenges. Most islands currently manage or must prepare for projected water shortages, for urbanization and changing rainfall patterns, high energy costs due to heavy reliance on imported energy, increasing land use conflicts from loss of land due to sea level rise and growing populations and control of invasive species that made outside effects on fragile island ecosystems.

To address these and other resource challenges, Hawaii has aggressively pursued a variety of policies to decrease reliance on imported energy, reduce overall energy use, more effectively use limited urban and suburban land and ensure future access to water for drinking, agricultural and other uses.

Hawaii is highly dependent upon imported fuels for energy. In 2011 the State imported 93 percent of its energy. Like many relatively small islands, uses mostly fuel oil to generate electricity. As a result Hawaii has historically had the highest electricity prices of any State, sometimes reaching 4 times the national average.

In order to reduce energy costs and encourage clean energy the State implemented a renewable energy goal of 40 percent by 2030 along with a goal of reducing total energy demand by 30 percent by 2030. We are also beginning to pursue strategies to reuse and recycle water and to use water more efficiently. Different islands in the State confront different challenges and opportunities in meeting their energy, water and land use needs.

The challenges are most acute on Oahu where over 70 percent of our State's 1.4 million residents live. So we must simultaneously pursue different energy and resource conservation strategies. Hawaii's water supplies as well as many other Pacific Island supplies are highly dependent upon rainfall and are threatened by increased hotter and drier weather, the loss of watershed forests and encroachment by rising sea level.

Nearly 50 percent of Hawaii's water supply comes from ground water sources and the rest come in from the approximately 376 streams that flow throughout the year. Ground water, which is also used for agricultural, industrial and domestic purposes is the principle source of municipal water supplies in Hawaii. All of these characteristics of our State and other island communities mean that we have to be especially careful stewards of our precious resources. Decisions we make today, especially as we face a changing climate and all that comes with it, will have a major impact on our future.

The goal of this hearing is to understand more deeply the challenges that Hawaii and other Pacific Islands face, highlight our successes, identify future opportunities and understand how the State can work more closely with the Federal Government to advance its goals.

We have 2 panels today.

Our first witness is Governor Neil Abercrombie. Governor Abercrombie will be followed by Mr. Julian Morimoto from Roosevelt High School and Ms. Julia Valentino Jimenez from Mililani.

Thank you all for being here and welcome.

Governor Abercrombie.

STATEMENT OF HON. NEIL ABERCROMBIE, GOVERNOR, STATE OF HAWAII, HONOLULU, HI; ACCOMPANIED BY JACKIE KOZAK THIEL, SUSTAINABILITY COORDINATOR

Mr. ABERCROMBIE. Thank you.

Senator SCHATZ. Thank you for being here. Let's start with you and move down the line.

Mr. ABERCROMBIE. Thank you very much.

Senator SCHATZ. I'm told to tell you to take 5 minutes for your testimony, but I'm pretty sure that staff will understand.

[Laughter.]

Mr. ABERCROMBIE. Thank you very much, Senator. It is a pleasure for me to be here with these 2 fine, young people, who are 3 dimensional embodiment of the future that you referred to.

I have a copy of the letter that you sent me to me where it says, very specifically, please limit oral summation of your written testimony to 5 minutes. So you did, I move. Everybody knows that I was coming prepared.

[Laughter.]

Mr. ABERCROMBIE. So I thank you very much for that opportunity. A point of fact, I would like to submit for the record, with your permission, formal testimony for the field hearing which I have before me and would like to summarize if I might.

Senator SCHATZ. Yes, please.

Mr. ABERCROMBIE. For you.

So that I would like to submit.

I would like to submit as well for the record, with your kind permission, a packet of material which has been shared with the President's Task Force on Climate Change and Resiliency including the work of our sustainability coordinator, Jackie Kozak Thiel, entitled, Navigating Change, Hawaii's approach to adaptation.

This was, in fact, a report for the first meeting of the State, Local and Tribal Leaders Task Force on climate preparedness and resilience in December of last year which we've been following up on. It includes our resolutions from the Hawaii Invasive Species Council which, I think, directly, again, addresses some of the points that you have raised. Our initiative here in the State on the rain follows the forest which is our Department of Land and Natural Resources approach to water conservation and preservation, if you will, in the midst of the global climate change and warming phenomenon.

Again, with your permission, please?

Senator SCHATZ. Yes.

Mr. ABERCROMBIE. Mr. Chairman.

Senator SCHATZ. These will be a part of the record.

Mr. ABERCROMBIE. Thank you so much.

In summary, I would like to in reference to the term, testimony, just refer you to page 2, if you have a copy of it there. Just with one little reference, if I might that speech to the particular necessities associated with being in the Asian Pacific region. As you know and as you are well aware of and as you've stated yourself on many occasions, we are Island People. We regard the Pacific Ocean as not separating us in the Asian Pacific region, but connecting us in the Asian Pacific region.

If you'll go to the paragraph on climate change on page 2, you'll notice with, recognizing this, that islands are windows to the future. The State of Hawaii has become the first sub national government to sign onto the Majuro Declaration for Climate Leadership along with the U.S. and Pacific Island nations.

I hope it doesn't seem presumptuous to other people that a State would sign into, sign onto, ask permission to sign onto a national treaty, in effect. The Declaration indicates that climate leadership is what is necessitated, particularly for island nations and for those nations that border the Asian Pacific region. Cite that because we do believe that Hawaii is a microcosm for global sustainability challenges and solutions.

When I first ran for office, Senator, in 1974, when I first ran for the State legislature, I should say, for the seat which you subsequently occupy, I made water and its conservation the principle element of my campaign. At the time it was thought to be an odd focus, thought to be a little bit abstract for a local legislative contest, if you will. But I didn't think so. I thought we were vulnerable. I thought we were vulnerable on the energy side, the food side, the natural resource and affordability of all of these aspects.

So going back then all the way to that time, to the present, this has been on the front line of concern for Hawaiians. Climate change and global warming has brought this to a higher degree of perception, publicly, I think, than ever before.

So we see, our islands, as a test bed for innovation. We're very, very grateful for the opportunity that you sit on, on this very valuable committee, in terms of its potential benefit for and your opportunity to make genuine progress, not only for our islands, but for the nation.

This enables us to have an integrated approach with that which the Federal Government is able to do for our Federal partnerships then are key. So we're committed to action on the Hawaii Clean Energy Initiative, on climate change and what we propose for the future which the testimony elaborates on at greater length than I have time for right now, our Aloha Plus Challenge for Sustainability.

Back there in 1974 we called it carrying capacity. That's transformed itself, I guess, in nomenclature to sustainability. It comes to the same thing.

Just let me elucidate a moment or 2 on those 3 elements, our Hawaii Clean Energy Initiative, of which you were a key element when you were Lieutenant Governor. 70 percent clean energy by 2030. The recognition of the oil import crosses of over 4, between $4 and $5 billion.

We propose to be a national leader in energy efficiency. We're, right now, we're ahead of schedule to meet our renewable goals. Our Federal partnerships will help us with a smart grid and storage and transportation elements all associated with that.

On climate change itself I've already mentioned that the President's Task Force on Climate Preparedness and Resilience. Again, I'm aided in this with the very able assistance of Jackie Thiel and the various departments of our State government that are committed to that.

We thank you for your leadership in the Congress on this issue. I'm glad in the time that you've been there, you've been recognized for that, not only with your committee assignment, but with your chairmanship of the subcommittee.

This is a priority issue, climate change for Hawaii, across the whole Pacific, as I indicated. We are hopeful that the recommendations that we will be forwarding to the President are—we know that they're the result of activities and action that we're taking here in Hawaii. We think it's applicable across the nation.

So we're taking climate change seriously. We already are experiencing the impacts, that's for certain. So we want to share what we're able to learn and what we're able to do with everyone across the country.

Finally, in this area, I mentioned this Aloha Plus Challenge. Without going into too much detail, that will be forthcoming in the days and weeks to come.

Your conference yesterday was about making sustainability happen. So leaders have to make commitments to act together to put policies into place that provide direction and incentivize.

So Hawaii was invited by the Global Island Partnership to make an international commitment to sustainability. We certainly accept that invitation. We're working with the mayors throughout the, the mayors and councils throughout the islands and the chair and members of the Office of Hawaiian Affairs to bring that about.

The Aloha Plus Challenge will set targets for 2030. This goes beyond political. In other words, we're not trying to make this oriented toward a political timeframe, but rather the timeframe necessary for us to address these serious issues. The Aloha Plus Challenge will deal with clean energy, global food production, natural resource management and invasive species prevention, waste production, smart growth and climate resilience and green jobs creation and education. All, I think, clearly the heart of the subject matter of the conference yesterday and your hearing today.

So we'll be announcing some details with regards to the Aloha Challenge, the Aloha Plus Challenge. We'll be working with the public and private sector to—for Hawaii's green growth. Of course, we're going to support the United State's Department of State in the upcoming United Nations Conference in Samoa on island sustainability.

So, Mr. Chairman, we have in the written testimony some more specific recommendations, a few more general recommendations based on my summary.

We can't build sustainable futures alone. We know that. We need private investment. We need private support. We need public support. We intend to try and bring that about.

We're committed, I can assure you, to being a model for integrated sustainability. We invite the Nation and the world to learn with us, not necessarily from us, but with us. We want to join with everyone as a part of that commitment.

I want to inform you that we're working very, very hard. Hope to have an answer, perhaps, within a month's time from the World Conservation Congress in 2016. It's never been held in the United States before. I think we're down to, perhaps, 2 sites. We've had a very successful site visit from the team from the Conservation Congress. This is entirely compatible with the goals of this conference and this hearing.

But we think that Hawaii has something unique to offer. I hope they conclude the same.

Also, you had yesterday the advantage and the opportunity to hear from Nainoa Thompson. The Hokule'a World Wide Voyage,

Mr. Chairman, I think summarizes what I have to say today. I think summarizes what the commitment of everyone here is all about. I hope gives a clear direction to the activities associated with the past 2 days.

This is the message of Aloha. This is the message that our diversity in this world should define us rather than divide us as we say here. I am happy to be able to recite to those who wonder what the message of Hawaii is that the aloha spirit, in fact, unites us as the Pacific Ocean unites us as brothers and sisters. That this message is something that should be taken not just to our friends and neighbors on the mainland in the United States and throughout the United States, but it's one, I think, that can usefully be taken to the world.

As part of the packet then, Mr. Chairman, I've included for the formal inclusion in the testimony I hope our Aloha law, the State law, HRS 5-7.5 which is in fact the Aloha spirit, the kindness, the unity, the realness, the pleasantness, the humility and the patience expressed with perseverance that represents aloha. I know that your activities here today are an expression of that. I thank you for the opportunity to be able to present this summary and to share with you, not only our State's priorities, but our aloha for you and all you're trying to accomplish.

Senator SCHATZ. Thank you very much.

Mr. ABERCROMBIE. Mahalo, very much.

[The prepared statement of Mr. Abercrombie follows:]

PREPARED STATEMENT OF HON. NEIL ABERCROMBIE, GOVERNOR, STATE OF HAWAII, HONOLULU, HI

Aloha Chair Schatz and Subcommittee members. As the Governor of the State of Hawaiʻi, I thank you for the opportunity to testify about our State's sustainability goals and how existing and new partnerships with Congressional leaders and the Federal Government can strengthen our ambitious efforts.

As isolated islands, Hawaiʻi is a microcosm of the sustainability challenges facing the planet. We import 80-90 percent of our food and energy, impacting our economy more than $8 billion each year. Hawaiʻi is the endangered species capital of the U.S, and we join other Pacific Islands on the frontlines of climate change. Despite our alarming vulnerability, Hawaiʻi has a distinct vantage point at the crossroads of the Asia-Pacific region and a unique opportunity to serve as a model for integrated, whole system solutions to these challenges. Our island perspective and indigenous host culture naturally leads to interconnected thinking and collaboration, and we are committed to developing nexus solutions for energy, water, waste, agriculture, natural resources, and community design.

Today, I will highlight three major initiatives with strong statewide support that illustrate Hawaiʻi's achievements, aspirations, and commitment to action:

- Excellent early progress on the Hawaiʻi Clean Energy Initiative;
- Our emerging national and international role in climate change leadership; and
- The Aloha+ Challenge: our shared leadership commitment to build a more resilient, sustainable and secure economy across our islands with six ambitious sustainability targets for 2030.

Hawaiʻi Clean Energy Initiative

As the most fossil fuel dependent state in the nation with $4.5 billion in annual outlays from our historical addiction to oil, clean energy is a matter of security and resilience in Hawaiʻi. The Hawaiʻi Clean Energy Initiative, jointly led by the State of Hawaiʻi and the U.S. Department of Energy, is a perfect example of how federal partnerships have helped to advance our state goal of 70 percent clean energy by 2030 through 40 percent renewable energy and 30 percent energy efficiency. In 2013, my Administration announced our commitment to go beyond 40 percent renewable. The clean energy sector has set the pace in Hawaiʻi. I am proud to report that we are currently at 18 percent renewable, beating our interim 2015 goal of 15 percent ahead of schedule. With the highest energy costs in the U.S., and as a national leader in energy efficiency and a pioneer in the frontier of renewable energy penetration into the grid, Hawai'i is uniquely positioned to serve as an international clean energy test bed and a model of Federal-State and Federal-Island partnerships.

Climate Change

Clean energy transformation is paramount for mitigating the impacts of climate change. I appreciate the Senate's leadership on climate change, including the Up all Night event in Washington D.C. organized by Hawai'i's Senator Schatz and others. I have been honored to share Hawai'i's perspectives as a member of President Obama's State, Local, and Tribal Leaders Task Force on Climate Preparedness and Resilience. At the first Task Force meeting, I presented a special report called Navigating Change-Hawai'i's Approach to Adaptation, which outlines our distinct challenges, solutions, and initial recommendations. Every region of our nation is represented on the Task Force, and I assure you that climate change is a priority issue for all of us. Governor Calvo of Guam and I have highlighted the special urgency of climate impacts on island communities and indigenous populations, including more severe storm events, less rainfall and fresh water, proliferation of invasive species, rising temperatures, ocean acidification, and sea level rise. Islands are windows into the future. With this recognition, the State of Hawai'i became the first sub-national government to sign onto the Majuro Declaration for Climate Leadership alongside the U.S. and Pacific Island nations.

Task Force members are developing recommendations for the President to help strengthen Federal support for State, Local, and Tribal efforts in disaster management, community health and development, natural resources and agriculture, and built systems and infrastructure. Through our Resilient Hawai'i Forums & surveys, we engaged over 1,000 citizens to identify diverse concerns and suggestions. The message is clear-the people of Hawai'i are taking climate change seriously and want to see action at every level of government. This is no longer about projections. We are already seeing the impacts in Hawai'i. Ranchers are struggling with drought. Our world-renowned beaches are disappearing due to erosion. Federal support is critical to help us understand, mitigate, and adapt to the impacts of climate change.

Hawai'i's major recommendations to the Task Force encourage greater flexibility for adaptive, place-based responses. We also call for stronger, ongoing horizontal coordination across federal agencies and vertical coordination with State, Local, and Tribal governments to ensure cost-effective alignment of proactive efforts and integration of programs. Additionally, in order to make adaptation-planning decisions, Hawai'i and other islands need adequate spatial and temporal resolution for modeling climate projections. Like many islands and coastal states, much of Hawai'i's critical infrastructure is located along the coast. We will need federal assistance in identifying vulnerable assets and strategies for decentralization and relocation.

Hawai'i is uniquely positioned to serve as a hub for coordinating domestic and international climate change efforts in the Asia-Pacific region. We recommend that the East-West Center be considered as a venue for an International Climate Change Resilience Forum. As home base to the U.S. Pacific Command, the State of Hawai'i also has the opportunity to build strong partnerships with the U.S. Department of Defense for building climate resilience in the region.

As a Task Force member, I will produce a report of Hawai'i's full list of detailed recommendations and plan to share them with our Congressional delegation for consideration before the end of the year.

Aloha+ Challenge—He Nohona 'Ae 'Oia-A Culture of Sustainability

The intent of this hearing is to examine successes and challenges of meeting sustainability goals. The State of Hawai'i has made sustainability a priority in our State Planning Act and incorporated an official definition, goals, and principles into law. Last year, I accepted the invitation from the Global Island Partnership to the State of Hawai'i to make an international commitment to sustainability in 2014 and to share and learn with other islands. It has been a pleasure to work with our four Mayors and the Chair of the Office of Hawaiian Affairs to develop the Aloha+ Challenge, our shared leadership commitment to 2030 targets in clean energy, local food production, natural resource management, waste reduction, smart growth, climate resilience, green jobs creation, and education. This effort is supported by our State Legislature and a cross-section of public and private sector leaders in Hawai'i Green Growth. We plan to formally launch the Aloha+ Challenge in the next few months with a joint, statewide commitment to:

    1. Clean Energy—70 percent clean energy, including 40 percent from renewables and 30 percent from efficiency

2. Local Food—Double the local food production with a goal of 20-30 percent of food consumed being grown locally

3. Natural Resource Management—Reverse the trend of natural resource loss mauka to makai by increasing watershed protection, community-based marine management, invasive species prevention and control, and restoration of native species

4. Waste Reduction—Reduce the solid waste stream prior to disposal by 50 percent through source reduction, recycling, and bioconversion

5. Smart Sustainable Communities—Increase livability and resilience in the built environment through planning and implementation at the state and county levels

6. Green Workforce—Increase local green jobs and education to implement these targets

Federal partnerships and support are crucial to progress on all six targets. I will highlight a few key successes, challenges, and opportunities for federal support of the Aloha+ Challenge targets.

Clean Energy

To guide Hawai'i's clean energy revolution, my Administration established a statewide energy policy in 2013 with five key elements: (1) diversifying our energy portfolio; (2) connecting the islands through integrated, modernized grids; (3) balancing technological, economic, environmental, and cultural considerations; (4) leveraging our international status as a clean energy test bed; and (5) allowing the market to pick winners.

We have a strong start on Hawai'i's clean energy transformation, but future gains will require even smarter solutions. Continued state and federal investments in analysis, planning, and infrastructure are required to catalyze the clean energy revolution. We greatly appreciate our successful MOU with the U.S. Department of Energy, which has provided vital support for Hawai'i to meet our 2030 statutory clean energy goals while reducing greenhouse gas emissions.

Due to this success, Hawai'i is keenly focused on removing barriers for renewable energy penetration by interconnecting our Oahu and Maui grids and improving grid infrastructure at the energy consumer/distribution and transmission levels. It is critical to ensure that dedicated funding is continued in order to commit resources to both short and long-term initiatives required to achieve Hawai'i's clean energy goals.

Partnerships and assistance in the following areas will also help to support Hawai'i's clean energy target:

1. Developing definitive, accurate renewable energy resource assessments on each island that consider technical constraints, costs, the environment, and community support and benefit.

2. Building a clear set of scenarios based on the island-based renewable energy resource assessments.

3. Working with utilities to develop methods to address curtailment risk as renewable energy penetration forces limitations at the substation, circuit and system level. This would include pursuing specific paths towards grid modernization, smart grid—advanced metering infrastructure; storage; alternative fuels like natural gas; and submarine transmission.

4. Developing a transportation plan, starting with a design charrette of local stakeholders to assess options for reducing large volumes of petroleum-based gasoline, diesel, jet fuel and marine fuels with a focus on policies and actions that can be achieved in Hawai'i through a roadmap and supporting analyses of costs, benefits, and sources of funding.

Local Food Production and Water

Part of my New Day Plan is to spark an Agricultural Renaissance in Hawai'i. The Waimea Nui Agricultural Complex project, with a Veteran to Farmer program, is a great example of our creative Food Self-Sufficiency Strategy in action. The complex will also include a biodigester that will create energy for a kitchen and processing facility where farmers can create value-added products to increase their revenue stream. This project would greatly benefit from additional support from USDA.

As the emergency drought in California underscores, water and food security are vitally linked. Federal partnerships can help us in both increasing our efficiencies in agricultural irrigation practices and reclaiming storm water, grey water, and rainwater to replace potable water in urban and agricultural applications.

Invasive Species

Invasive species are one of the top threats to Hawai'i's agriculture, natural resources, and human health. I have directed my departments to effectively work across silos through the interagency Hawai'i Invasive Species Council. We recently passed resolutions urging federal agencies to support Hawai'i's efforts to strengthen biosecurity. The resolutions are attached with opportunities for partnership with the U.S. Departments of Agriculture, Interior, and Defense.

The State of Hawai'i would also like to be considered as one of the U.S. Department of Agriculture's pilot sites to create a harmonized national systems approach to nursery certification.

Natural Resource Management

Healthy forests, wetlands, coral reefs, and other natural ecosystems are critical to sustainability and resilience in a changing climate. In 2011, my Administration unveiled a plan to replenish Hawai'i's source of water through the Rain Follows the Forest Watershed Initiative. In 2013, we updated our Ocean Resources Management Plan to identify management priorities and interagency implementation actions. We need healthy watersheds and reefs to continue to deliver fresh water, absorb greenhouse gases, control runoff and erosion, protect shorelines from storm surge, produce sustainable seafood, maintain our unique biodiversity, and provide other natural benefits that allow us to survive and thrive in the middle of the Pacific Ocean.

Federal partnerships and support have been critical in matching our state investment in natural resource management, such as the U.S. Fish and Wildlife Service's Cooperative Endangered Species Recovery Fund and State Wildlife Grant program. A restoration of these funds (to FY2011 and FY2014 levels respectively) would help Hawai'i to make progress on simultaneously protecting water supply, preserving biodiversity, and preparing for the impacts of climate change through ecosystem-based adaptation.

Waste Reduction

Solid waste management is a unique challenge in Hawai'i because we are a geographically-isolated island state. Currently, we import the vast majority of goods used in the state, which in turn creates waste that requires management. Hawai'i has developed a variety of innovative waste management systems to address the state's solid waste issues, including development of H-Power (Honolulu Program of Waste Energy Recovery), the Deposit Beverage Container Program (HI-5), the Advance Disposal Fee Program for glass, and electronic waste recycling.

In order to meet our 2030 target of reducing our solid waste stream by 50 percent, Hawai'i needs federal assistance to:

1. Establish a market for recycled products
2. Reduce the level of packaging in transported goods
3. Establish standardized best practices for manufacturing that will create less waste

All these measures would be useful to other jurisdictions that are also working to reduce waste.

Smart Sustainable Communities

Ninety percent of our state's population lives on this island. We need to make sure that our urban and rural communities are resilient, livable, and age-friendly. Transit-oriented development is a central component to sustainable community design and smart growth. Interagency programs like the HUD-DOT-EPA Sustainable Communities Partnership should be replicated and expanded to encourage innovation, collaboration, and performance monitoring at a state and local level. In order to better incentivize sustainable community design throughout the country, we need to better align transportation costs and usage. As the Federal Highway Trust Fund decreases from the reduction of vehicle miles travels (VMT) and increased fuel efficiency, we need to transition from a fixed cost system to a variable cost system that accounts for VMT. A VMT pricing system could be used in place of the existing gas tax system and help to pay for new resilient infrastructure. This approach would support performance measures for all modes of transportation and broader community goals that link land use, community design, health, safety, equity, and environmental sustainability.

Education—Student participation on the witness panel today demonstrates the importance of empowering the next generation of leaders through education. We need to make sure that our children are obtaining the 21st century skills and multidisciplinary knowledge from pre-school through higher education. This is a key investment in the integrated sustainability solutions of the future.

Green Jobs—As we strive toward all of these targets, we will create a diversified workforce through the economic and entrepreneurial opportunities presented by solving these challenges. Hawaiʻi is already one of the top states in the nation for clean energy job growth.

Government cannot and should not build a sustainable future alone. Private sector investment, innovations, and partnerships are critical. Government's key role is to reduce risk, increase market reliability, and strategically leverage government funding to mobilize major private finance. The combination of clean energy policies in the Hawaiʻi Clean Energy Initiative and Hawaiʻi's Energy Excelerator is a powerful example of this approach. $10 million in federal funding leveraged over $55 million in private sector investment and resulted in over 400 green jobs. There are similar entrepreneurial opportunities in agriculture, natural resource management, waste reduction, and green building that would benefit from federal investment and incentives.

Yesterday's Ascent Conference at the University of Hawaiʻi reflects the type of integrated thinking and public-private solutions that are needed to meet the sustainability challenges in Hawaiʻi and around the world. Hawaiʻi is ready to serve as a model of integrated and innovative approaches that can be scaled up for national and international benefit. We welcome others to learn with us.

The Hōkūleʻa, the traditional Hawaiian voyaging canoe, is embarking on the Worldwide Voyage to share Hawaiʻi's sustainability message around the globe and carry lessons learned from other ports and places with a focus on ocean connections. We are working closely with the U.S. Department of State to help represent our country at the upcoming United Nations Conference for Small Island Developing States focused on island sustainability in September 2014 in Samoa. In 2016, we hope to be the first U.S. location to host the World Conservation Congress, where we will showcase real progress on all our Aloha+ Challenge targets.

My Administration is committed to leading sustainability efforts through interagency coordination, public-private partnerships, and strategic investments. The State of Hawaiʻi sincerely appreciates collaboration with the Federal Government to advance our 2030 targets. I thank you for your leadership to elevate the pressing issues of climate change and sustainability in Congress and for the opportunity to highlight Hawaiʻi's priorities.

Senator SCHATZ. Thank you, Governor.
Ms. Jimenez.

STATEMENT OF JULIA VALENTINO JIMENEZ, ROOSEVELT HIGH SCHOOL, HONOLULU, HI

Ms. JIMENEZ. Good afternoon.

My name is Julia Jimenez. I'm a homeschooled senior, who has had the privilege of being a part of the Schatz Senior program. I'd like to thank Chairman Senator Schatz for allowing me to speak before the committee today.

As the next generation to join the work force and venture out into the world, we have a vested interest on the issues of climate change and sustainability. We see these problems. We see our future. For truly these problems are our future.

If nothing is done now, it is my generation that will have to pick up the pieces. That is why I am here today, to urge Congress to address these problems while we still can. For it is much easier to move a vase away from the edge than to glue it back together once it has been broken.

Although climate change and sustainability may be important issues that are often talked about, I found that people of the community truly don't understand the depth of the problem. In my own circles of family and friends very, very few even recognize that climate change is actually happening. There is a certain ignorance or denial that allows people to turn a blind eye.

Before we can begin to solve climate change and prevent an unsustainable future we must recognize that there's something to change and prevent. Congress must partner with the communities to make a true difference. In order to do this education must be a priority, for citizens and businesses alike.

I recommend that Congress invest in research on what is the best way to reach the communities whether that be through unbiased curriculum in the schools or innovative outreach programs.

Another recommendation would be for Congress to set up an incentive plan so that companies would be encouraged to educate their customers about sustainable technologies. If these environmentally conscious products were introduced into our lives I believe it would not only educate citizens but encourage them to take an active role in a sustainable future.

Climate change is primarily caused by greenhouse gases that are often caused by the emission of carbon dioxide after its source has been used for fuel for certain technologies. Last night former Vice President, Al Gore, said a wonderful quote, saying, "It is like we decided to use the atmosphere as an open sewage line for gas waste." He also compared the pollution of human kind to releasing 400,000 Hiroshima bombs in 24 hours. This is why it is up to us to keep careful watch of our own carbon footprints as individuals and as a Nation.

A program is being created in Hawaii called Ka Hei. This program allows schools to become environmentally conscious and sustainable while reducing the carbon footprints of the infrastructures themselves. This program sets us a clear plan toward sustainability and green energy including the goals of reducing costs in 255 DOE schools, implementing sustainability and energy efficiency, supporting the goal of 90 percent clean energy by 2040 and having more educational opportunities concerning sustainability and stimulating the economy through local construction labor.

Even though this program was created for schools it is not limited to that capacity.

I would like to recommend for the committee to set in place Federal incentives for companies, offices and schools implement plans similar to this.

Too often do I walk into a government building and see the old school lights that hike up electricity costs and the use of desktop computers when the use of laptops could save more energy. It is for this reason that I would recommend the committee put forth a timeline for government buildings to become more cost effective and energy efficient and diminish their own carbon footprint.

When we talk of such massive issues as climate change and sustainability every bit of help counts. If we, as a nation, can commit to adapting our infrastructures to be environmentally conscious I believe that we can make a true difference in the fight against climate change.

For years I lived in a city called Bakersfield in California. Bakersfield is surrounded by a horseshoe of mountains where smog will come to sit. This created a horrible air quality that actually affected my lung capacity and gave me breathing problems. No one wants our beautiful island to become like this nor do we want our nation to become like this. That is why climate change is such an important issue, not only for our generation, but also for your generation now.

Thank you again to Senator Schatz for allowing myself and my fellow intern to testify today. We are grateful that Congress and the committee is dedicated to addressing climate change and sustainability for the actions that you do now will affect our future.

Thank you.

[The prepared statement of Ms. Jimenez follows:]

PREPARED STATEMENT OF JULIA VALENTINO JIMENEZ, ROOSEVELT HIGH SCHOOL, HONOLULU, HI

Good afternoon. My name is Julia Jimenez and I am a homeschooled senior who has the privilege of being a part of the Schatz Seniors program. I would like to thank Chairman Senator Schatz for allowing me to speak today before the committee.

As the next generation to join the work force and venture out into the world, we have a vested interest on the issues of climate change and sustainability. We see these problems and we see our future, because truly these problems are our future. If nothing is done now, it is my generation that will be left to try and pick up the pieces. That is why I am here today: to urge Congress to address these problems while we still can. It is much easier to move a vase away from the edge then to glue it back together again.

Although climate change and sustainability may be an important issues that are often talked about, I have found that people of the community truly don't understand the depth of the problem. In my own circles of friends and family, very, very few even recognize that climate change is happening. There is a certain ignorance or denial that allows people to turn a blind eye. Before we can begin to try to solve climate change and prevent an unsustainable future, we must first recognize that there is something to solve and prevent. Congress must partner with communities to make a true difference. And in order to do this, education must be a priority, for citizens and businesses. I recommend that Congress invest in research on what is the best way to reach the communities, whether that be through more unbiased curriculum in schools or innovative outreach programs. Another recommendation would be for Congress to set up an incentive plan, so companies would be encouraged to educate their customers about sustainable technologies. If these environmentally conscious products were introduced in our lives, I believe it would not only educate citizens, but encourage them to take an active role in a sustainable future.

Climate Change is primarily caused by greenhouse gasses, which are often caused by the emission of carbon dioxide after its source has been used as fuel for certain technologies. That is why it is up to us to keep careful watch of our own carbon footprints, as individuals and as a nation. A program is being created in Hawaii call Ka Hei. This program allows schools to become environmentally conscious and sustainable, by reducing the carbon footprint of the infrastructures themselves. This program sets up a clear plan towards sustainability and green energy, including the goals of reducing costs of 255 DOE schools, implementing sustainability and energy efficiency, supporting the goal of 90 percent clean energy by 2040, having more educational opportunities concerning sustainability, and stimulating the economy through local construction labor.

Even though this program was created for schools, it is not limited to that capacity. I would like to recommend for the Committee to set in place federal incentives for companies, offices, and schools to implement plans similar to Ka Hei. Too often do I walk into a government building and see the old-school lights that hike-up electricity costs, and the use of desktop computers when the use of laptops could save more energy. It is for this reason that I would recommend the Committee put forth a timeline for government buildings to put in place cost effective and energy efficient measures to diminish their carbon footprint. When we talk of such massive issues as in climate change and sustainability, every bit of help counts. If we as a nation could commit to adapting our infrastructures to be environmentally conscious, I believe we could make a true difference in the fight against climate change.

Thank you again to Senator Schatz for allowing myself and my fellow intern to testify today. We are grateful that Congress and the Committee are dedicated to addressing climate change and sustainability, as the actions you do now will affect our future.

Senator SCHATZ. Thank you very much.

Mr. Morimoto.

STATEMENT OF JULIAN MANGADLAO MORIMOTO, ROOSEVELT HIGH SCHOOL, HONOLULU, HI

Mr. MORIMOTO. Good afternoon. Good afternoon, everyone.

My name is Julian Morimoto. Before I begin I would like to thank Chairman Schatz and the Subcommittee on Water and Power today for taking the time to listen to our testimony. I'd also like to take this time to acknowledge my fellow interns in the audience. Interns, please wave. Because truly, without them, I would not have had the opportunity to be here today and discuss our efforts to create a better future for the State.

My fellow intern, Julia Jimenez and I, are grateful to be here today on behalf of the Schatz Seniors Program to testify on matters regarding sustainability efforts. How we, not as individuals, corporations or groups, but as a community, can finally bridge the dismal gap between ourselves and the brighter, greener, more sustainable future. My one wish is that after today we can all step out of this building with a clear vision for the future of our country.

The Schatz Seniors decided to undertake an innovative project to create a system that would rank schools in terms of their environmental friendliness. Hopefully once the system is finally complete it will serve as a model for schools in other States. We would like to share with you what we have been working on and where we plan to go with this in the future.

The purpose is to create an annual, publicized ranking system by which we can compare local high schools in terms of their sustainability. We decided that there were 3 main questions that needed to be answered.

One is already being done to rate the eco-friendliness of schools.

What should we propose be included in such criteria?

How would we implement such a system?

We then proceeded to collect information from schools, programs and institutions throughout the island.

The main 7 criteria proposed were energy usage, water waste diversion, educational opportunities, food services, responsible resource management, transportation and campus initiative.

In addition to these basic ideas some sample questions that would be needed to—that would need answers would be other courses offered that are dedicated to teaching students about sustainability and environmental awareness, other regular school sponsored events promoting environmental awareness and other active student led organizations dedicated to sustainable practices.

It is our hope that this will be implemented in both public, private and charter schools by 2016.

I present this project to you today in hopes that the Senate will take these programs to the next level. Instead of merely implementing them only in Hawaii why not expand and give schools throughout the United States the incentive to be greener both on campus and off campus. These incentives could include national awards and merits and will encourage schools they should want to take part in creating a sustainable future.

At the end of the day by providing incentives and deciding what makes up these criteria, the people of the United States will know that these issues are important and that our government is dedicated to them, to fixing them. Student engagement is critical to affecting change, developing leaders of the future and creating awareness of global, national and local issues also.

While we support Federal legislation such as Senator Boxer's Carbon Tax bill, we know that that effort will take time. However, as Senators, hosting conversations within their States can be done now and will make an impact.

Yesterday former Vice President, Al Gore, spoke to an audience of 9 thousand including over 4,000 students. More importantly the conversation and excitement continued as the students boarded buses and left for over 30 different schools. We strongly encourage the Senate to reach out to students and young people and engage them in meaningful conversations about sustainability.

By hosting summits, lectures and community conversations with students of all ages changing the vocabulary to explain technical and regulatory issues in easy to understand terms and avoiding acronyms.

Giving concrete examples that young people and their families can implement regardless of geography and income.

Keeping the message short and focused.

Also creating programs such as high school internships, school awards, contests that include and inspire students to get involved and learn.

The Gore lecture also proved to be a rather inviting and informative experience. We think that the 2 most important take aways are that there is hope. There is statistically significant evidence that suggests we are moving in a better direction. Furthermore, our actions today will affect the world we live in tomorrow.

Projects like the Green School Ranking System aren't just about breathing cleaner air and fixing climate change. As leaders it has been our obligation to not only better the world of today, but also to shape the world of tomorrow. We hope that eventually similar systems to the Green School Ranking will soon be implemented in other States and serve as sustainability models throughout the country.

Thank you once again.

[The prepared statement of Mr. Morimoto follows:]

PREPARED STATEMENT OF JULIAN MANGADLAO MORIMOTO, ROOSEVELT HIGH SCHOOL, HONOLULU, HI

Good afternoon everyone! My name is Julian Morimoto, and before I begin I would like to thank Senator Brian Schatz, Governor Neil Abercrombie, the Senate Committee on Energy and Natural Resources, and all the witnesses present today who took the time to hear our testimonies. I'd also like to take this time to acknowledge my fellow interns in the audience (interns please wave to the rest of the audience); for without their hard work, I would not have had the spectacular opportunity to stand here today and discuss our efforts to create a better future for this wondrous state. My fellow intern, Julia Jimenez, and I are gratefully here on behalf of the Schatz Seniors' program to testify on matters regarding sustainability efforts and how we—not as individuals, corporations, or groups, but as a community—can finally bridge the dismal gap between ourselves and the brighter, greener, more sustainable future. My one wish, is that after today, we can all step out of this building with a clearer vision for the future of our glorious country.

The Schatz Seniors Program give high school students precious first-hand exposure to the areas of public policy and public administration. For me—and many others—this opportunity has been one of the highlights of my senior year. The program has greatly broadened our intellectual horizons, and given us skills we can use to continue positively impacting our community for years to come. This year, the Schatz Seniors embarked on a revolutionary journey to impact the way schools throughout Hawai'i integrate sustainability through curriculum, student-led programs, infrastructure, and community integration.

The project began when Senator Schatz learned colleges were being ranked in terms of their eco-friendliness. In this, he saw opportunity. He wondered if it would be possible for such a system to be implemented in Hawai'i to positively impact public educational institutions in the state of Hawai'i. The team captains of this project were seniors Erin Carroll, Kara Tanaka, and myself. We decided that there were three main questions which needed answers:

1. What is already being done to rate the eco-friendliness of schools?
2. What should we propose be included in such criteria?
3. How would we implement such a system?

We then proceeded to collect information from schools, programs, and institutions throughout the island. The main seven criteria we proposed were:
1. Energy usage
2. Waste diversion
3. Educational opportunities
4. Food services
5. Responsible resource management
6. Transportation
7. Campus initiative

I am sad to say, however, that our time as Schatz Seniors is almost over, and that we will have to leave the actual implementation of this system to the next group of Schatz Seniors; and I hope, that they will learn and grow just as much as we did throughout the course of this project.

I present this project to you today in hopes that you will take programs like these to the next level: instead of merely implementing them only in Hawai'i, why not expand, and give schools throughout the United States the incentive to be greener both on-campus and off-campus? These incentives could include national awards and merits, and will encourage schools nationwide to take part in creating a sustainable future. To the senate committee on energy and natural resources, perhaps you could also play a part in determining what should be taken into consideration when ranking schools around the nation. At the end of the day, by providing incentives and deciding what makes up these criteria, the people of the United States will know that these issues are important, and that our government is dedicated to fixing them.

Projects like the Green School Ranking aren't just about breathing cleaner air or fixing climate change. From the time I was old enough to count, my generation has always heard, "You are the leaders of tomorrow." Now, I stand here today, at the near-end of my high school career, finally beginning to understand what this meant. As leaders, it has been our obligation to not only better the world of today, but also to shape the world of tomorrow. My fellow interns and I each had our own reasons for taking part in this project, and I will share mine. I took part in this project because I wanted to ensure that twenty years from now, I can look into the pure eyes of a child and say, "You are a leader of tomorrow." knowing that he or she can learn and grow to be a remarkable individual in a greener, brighter, and greater country.

Senator SCHATZ. Thank you very much to the testifiers.

I'll start my questions for Governor Abercrombie.

Mr. ABERCROMBIE. Thank you.

Senator SCHATZ. Governor, I know you've been appointed to the President's Climate Task Force. I wonder whether you wouldn't mind giving us an update on how it's working, who comprises the task force and what their timeframe is in terms of providing a work product for some national policy changes?

Mr. ABERCROMBIE. I would be delighted to do that.

This is in the packet that I was providing to you. It's our report to the initial conference. The—it covers fresh water coastlines, ocean resources, security, culture, sensitivity to culture, actual information decisionmaking context, how to facilitate coordination, etcetera.

It involves, more formally, tribal leaders, mayors, council members, Governors, all across the country to try to address both the regional and national conditions and circumstances that are—that climate preparedness and resilience. It's not just a matter of addressing the idea that there is climate change, global warming, for which we have to be prepared for what to do in terms of being able to be resilient to do it.

The—there's been a meeting in Los Angeles and another coming up in Iowa. With your permission I'd like to give the opportunity to Jackie Thiel to summarize that for you because she is our Sustainability Coordinator. I think it would give you some of the details which show that this more than just a forum or an academic exercise, but an opportunity for us to move genuine recommendations forward for legislation.

Senator SCHATZ. Please, Ms. Thiel.

Ms. THIEL. Hello, Senator.

Thank you, Governor, for the opportunity to add.

It's been a great honor supporting our Governor in this role. He's one of only 8 Governors that were appointed to the task force. So it's a tremendous opportunity for Hawaii. Actually the Governor of Guam is another.

So I know this hearing is about Hawaii and other islands. So it's been great for Governor Abercrombie and Governor Calvo to bring the message of islands to this task force. They are 2 of 26 members. So as the Governor mentioned mayors and county commissioners are also involved.

The task force is focusing on 4 major areas of climate resilience. So, built systems which includes a lot of the things that we talked at ASCENT yesterday, the water/energy nexus, transportation, a lot of those built assets that we have there that are going impacted by sea level rise and other climate change impacts, also natural resources and agriculture, community health and developments.

We are really lucky in Hawaii that we don't have mosquito borne illnesses like malaria and dengue fever, but these have been identified as climate sensitive diseases.

Finally, disaster managements.

One thing that I think was really striking at our first meeting in DC is that many of the other task force members have recently suffered a disaster. They were there for super storm Sandy, for Irene, fires and floods and Fort Collins Mayor, Mayor Weitkunat spoke of that. So I think that Hawaii is really in a position to learn from these other places that have more recent disasters than we have.

Governor ABERCROMBIE. So one of the things we're doing then is having what we call resiliency forms here. Again maybe Jackie can elaborate a little bit on what we've already done and what we plan.

Ms. THIEL. So one of the things that the White House really asked us to do is that could only ask, you know, only appoint 26 members, was to really reach out and engage stakeholders in our region, in our States. So we've engaged over 1,000 citizens in Hawaii through online survey and Resilient Hawaii forms. One was during the Pacific Risk Management "Ohana Conference recently that NOAA. NOAA has been an amazing partner to us through this process, helping to support our resilient white forms. I think a great example of Federal partnerships.

Senator SCHATZ. So Governor, I have a question about——

Mr. ABERCROMBIE. Could I just add one point to that?

Senator SCHATZ. Go ahead.

Mr. ABERCROMBIE. It's a fact of nature. What do we do about rising water, for example? What we've gone through is proposals concerning reefs, concerning what we can do to deal with the question of rising water because it's one thing to talk about it in the abstract or in mega terms. It's another one, literally, every inch of our land mass is coastline. So and each island, within different regions and sections of the island, has its own issues associated with it.

So that's the kind of thing that that the resiliency forms are dealing with. We know that we don't have a cookie cutter approach that's going to work where one size fits all. It's going to have to be site specific and regional specific.

Senator SCHATZ. At the level of mayor and Governor and county commissioner is there bipartisan cooperation? Is there a recognition? You know, what I found even in the halls of the Senate is that if we talk about disaster preparedness, if we talk about severe weather, if we talk about civil defense, then I can find common cause with bipartisan dance partners.

I'm wondering with, in the context of this task force, if you can get mayors who are Republicans to participate as long as you're careful with your language?

Mr. ABERCROMBIE. Yes. Yes.

Let me put it this way. Disasters like Hurricane Sandy know no ideology. There is no political points to be scored.

The climate change, global warming, is no respecter of particular partisan interests. So that is well recognized that the language that we indicate is one of coordination and cooperation because these things are not isolated in political jurisdictions. A city boundary means absolutely nothing to a hurricane or a cyclone or a flood or a heat wave or as you probably experienced much to your great regret, more often than not, a freeze wave.

Senator SCHATZ. Polar vortex.

Mr. ABERCROMBIE. Polar vortex. Yes. Yes.

[Laughter.]

Mr. ABERCROMBIE. Another phrase that has been added to the mix.

So the short answer is yes. It is possible by focusing on what we have in common rather than what differences can be conjured on.

Senator SCHATZ. So one final question for the Governor and perhaps for your Assistant Building Coordinator before I move on to the students and allow you to get back to your work.

I'm interested, very much, in the progress that State and county governments are making here, but also nationally in energy efficiency performance contracting and would love it if you would talk a little bit about what State and I know the city and county of Honolulu has made good progress.

Mr. ABERCROMBIE. Yes.

Senator SCHATZ. Talk about how the economics have shifted in ways that provide us real opportunities?

Mr. ABERCROMBIE. Let me just give you a little example.

At the Honolulu International Airport we've signed a contract on energy efficiency and light that is going to save in 2013-2014 dollars, $10 of millions of dollars, perhaps into hundreds of millions of dollars by the time it's over by changing, simply by having a relentless approach to modernizing our technology, utilizing modern technology, in light. Just that alone saves money instantaneously. That's money that can be invested back into further activity in order to make everything work more efficiently.

That is going across the country. Our on bill financing to enable people to get energy efficiency through renewable energy, the resources that otherwise might not be possible in terms of financing. If you can pay it on your energy bill and pay it off just as if it was a mortgage, this is something that brings it down to the grass roots level and gives visible evidence to a family that they are not just subject to energy prices, the object of it, but rather that they can get control over their own lives, financially and otherwise.

What this does, in my judgment, is an opportunity for people then to say, look, I can do something about it. I'm not just the victim here. I'm not just an observer of something being done to me. I'm able to, not only participate, but take an active role and seem to then meet the energy challenge of this century.

Senator SCHATZ. Thank you very much, Governor, for providing your testimony.

Feel free to stay with the other testifiers, but if you have to——

Mr. ABERCROMBIE. Thank you.

Senator SCHATZ. Go, we understand.

Ms. Jimenez, I have a question for you about your—about people your age and their awareness of climate change as an issue. I'm wondering whether your average teenager is aware at all about this problem.

My sense is that young people in Hawaii care very much about the environment, but it tends to be more local intensity, more land use based intensity, more about your personal experience in the environment. As important as climate change is, I understand it's somewhat abstract for a 15 year old. I'm wondering whether my assessment is correct or whether the awareness is growing?

Ms. JIMENEZ. I would have to say that there definitely is a disconnect between what the teenagers of Hawaii, at least that I know, believe is happening and what is actually happening. There seems to be a problem of not truly understanding with that of the problem. It's not an issue that is in normal conversation, at least in my circles.

I would have to say that in my circles we are usually very politically competent. We keep up with the news. We know the legislatures. We actually go out and campaign. We discuss political topics on a day by day basis. The topic of sustainability has not come up once.

That's just something from my own personal experience of they're not understanding the true depth of the issue. I think that's why it's important for there to be a more integration of education for the teenage community in Hawaii on not just the overreaching issue of global warming and to go down to the more specifics of sustainability, specifically to water sustainability.

Senator SCHATZ. Thank you very much, Ms. Jimenez.

I have a question for Mr. Morimoto and then a question for both of you. This is my third question for both of you is purely to satisfy my own curiosity.

[Laughter.]

Senator SCHATZ. My question for you is what's happening from your standpoint because I know from the Department of Education's standpoint what's happening in environmental education. But I want you to tell me what's happening in environmental education at Roosevelt High School.

Mr. MORIMOTO. OK.

At Roosevelt High School we have a little garden by the Science Department building. I think it was a really cool innovation. Usually the Green Club goes and checks in on it. They really integrate themselves into learning how to properly take care of plants. I'm sure they also learn, like, what is also really harmful and detrimental to the growth of plant life in Hawaii.

What we also have is AP Environmental Science which that is also teaching young students how to play an active role in creating a better environment for their future.

A few years ago we had the Law and Leadership Academy. AP Environmental Science was one of the required presences. I'm assuming that the faculty knew that environmental issues were going to become a very integrated part of discussions of the modern world today.

Senator SCHATZ. Thank you very much. I appreciate that.

Let me just ask one final question for the both of you.

How do you and how do your peers get your information primarily?

Ms. JIMENEZ. My situation is a little unique since I am homeschooled. The greater majority of my friends are also homeschooled as well. So honestly we get our information just from regular news sources, just as an adult may.

We watch the news. We read newspapers. We talk about it amongst ourselves. It's honestly also the conversation that's going around us, what the adults are also talking about, we'll chime in with our own opinions.

We don't have the luxury of the public and private schools that have the classes integrated into the system. We have to go find our own information.

Senator SCHATZ. Mr. Morimoto, how luxurious is Roosevelt?

[Laughter.]

Senator SCHATZ. Where do you and your friends get your information?

I mean, obviously, your teachers. But I'm more interested in how you consume the news and how you get factual information.

Mr. MORIMOTO. In regards to daily life or regards to the Green School project?

Senator SCHATZ. I mean more generally in terms of what's happening in the world. Are you—is it social? Is it television and the newspaper like the rest of us? Is it mostly the web or where are you getting your information?

Mr. MORIMOTO. I believe that currently at my school at least what I've noticed over the years is that the medium of which information is transferred between individuals is very different. Comparing schools I know some schools are still using Facebook while others are, like, you know, Facebook was so 10 years ago.

[Laughter.]

Mr. MORIMOTO. With our——

[Laughter.]

Ms. JIMENEZ. Twitter and Tumblr.

Senator SCHATZ. Now you have his complete attention.

[Laughter.]

Mr. MORIMOTO. However, at Roosevelt the main media of communication is, in fact, social media.

The teachers are very integrated with their class, with their students. So they also share information as well.

Nowadays with smart phones, you may or may not already be aware of this, but a lot of us won't, no that's not right, but——

[Laughter.]

Mr. MORIMOTO. A lot of us have apps like CNN. So I get CNN reports on my phone very often throughout the day. I even got a few during yesterday's session which I didn't look at, obviously.

But those—that is also a really common media is through cell phones and social media. That can be mobile. Because that's what this world today is all about, right? Mobile. You're always on the go.

So if you really want to reach out to people of my age and hopefully for future generations. I will be out of touch 1 day, but until that day comes.

[Laughter.]

Mr. MORIMOTO. I think that going mobile. Going mobile and being integrated in that system is a great way to go.

Senator SCHATZ. Thank you.

Ms. JIMENEZ. If I may?

Senator SCHATZ. Sure, Ms. Jimenez and then we'll move on to the next panel.

Go ahead, please.

Ms. JIMENEZ. Going on with what he said. If you asked a 16/17 year old to sit down and watch an entire news program or documentary on climate change you will get glassed over eyes and a lot of texting.

[Laughter.]

Ms. JIMENEZ. But if you post on Facebook and you ask them to go look at Facebook they can do that.

If you ask them to go look at Twitter, they can do that and Tumblr and all of the other social media sites. It's something that we do daily. So that is definitely a way to reach the younger generation.

Senator SCHATZ. Thank you very much. We'll take your testimony——

Mr. ABERCROMBIE. Thank you for not asking me that question.

[Laughter.]

Senator SCHATZ. Thank you very much to the testifiers. We appreciate your testimony.

Ask the second panel to go ahead and sit at the testifier's table.

Mr. ABERCROMBIE. Thank you, Chairman.

Senator SCHATZ. With us today we have Hermina Morita, Chair of the Hawaii Public Utilities Commission.

Dawn Lippert, Director of the Energy Excelerator in Hawaii.

Wendy Meguro, Assistant Professor of Sustainable Buildings and Community Design at the University of Hawaii, Sea Grant Program.

Harrison Rue, County Building and TOD Administrator for the City and County of Honolulu, Department of Planning and Permitting.

Bill Tam, Deputy Director of the Commission on Water Resource Management, Department of Land and Natural Resources.

Dr. Stephen Pauley, President of the E.W. Pauley Foundation.

Thank you all for being here. Your written testimony will be included in the record. So please take about 5 minutes to summarize your main points.

Ms. Morita, we'll start with you and move down the line.

STATEMENT OF HERMINA M. MORITA, CHAIR, HAWAII PUBLIC UTILITIES COMMISSION, HONOLULU, HI

Ms. MORITA. Thank you, Senator.

So I'll just get straight to the point.

You know, last October I had the privilege of participating in a State efficiency and renewable power policy roundtable which was convened by the former Chair of the Senate Committee on Energy and Natural Resources, Jeff Bingaman and the former Secretary of State, George Schultz at Stanford's Steyer-Taylor Center for Energy Policy and Finance. The roundtable included the Chairs from 4 States, the PEC Chairs from 4 States, Hawaii, Kansas, Texas and Washington and the Chair of the New York State Energy Research and Development Authority. It was an effort to identify which State level energy policies have proven to be the most effective and which ones have succeeded and ultimately which policies can attract bipartisan support to help mitigate climate change.

My understanding is the report should be out this summer.

The roundtable discussion was focused in 4 areas.

Renewables.

Energy Efficiency.

Customer Generation.

Financing Mechanisms.

So I'm going to focus in these 4 areas so you have a basis for comparisons with other States when the report becomes available.

So the first is renewable energy. We are on track to exceed our 2015 renewable portfolio standards target of 15 percent and expected to meet our 2020 target of 25 percent.

The Hawaiian electric companies have achieved a consolidated RPS of 34.4 percent in 2013. But remember this includes energy efficiency savings as well as solar water heating technologies.

So excluding those types of energy savings the HECO Company's renewable energy generation percentage is at 18.2 percent.

The 2013 RPS report for the Kauai Island Utility Cooperative has not been filed with the Commission yet. However, KIUC increased its percentage from 14.69 percent in 2011 to 16.64 percent in 2012. They anticipate to have online by 2015 an additional 24 megawatts of photovoltaics and 6.7 megawatts of biomass. That's pretty amazing for a utility with a system peak of approximately 76 megawatts.

Regarding energy efficiency.

Hawaii's energy efficiency portfolio standards mandate target is 43 hundred gigawatt/hours electric use reduction by 2030. Hawaii is on track to achieve more than 1,550 gigawatt hours in savings by 2015. That exceeds our internal target by more than 12 percent.

Hawaii Energy, the ratepayer funded energy efficiency services provider which administers the public benefit fee, is an essential component of the State's efforts to capture untapped energy efficiency resources contributing more than 80 percent of the energy savings achieved since 2009. In the program year ending June 30th, 2013 Hawaii Energy programs will deliver 1.4 billion kilowatt/hours in lifetime savings at a total program cost of 2.3 cents per kilowatt/hours. This, in turn, will save an estimated equivalent of 2.4 million barrels of oil and 1.2 million tons of greenhouse gas emissions.

At an average electricity price of 30.7 cents per kilowatt/hours customers will save approximately 450 million dollars on their electricity bills over the life of the installed efficiency measures.

With regard to customer generation.

Hawaii's electric utilities lead the Nation in the installation of group photovoltaics relative to the size of our island grids. Since 2005 Hawaii has seen exponential growth in the amount of PV installed on each island and the level of PV capacity relative to the demand on each island is approaching 20 percent.

Senator, when we passed the 2001 net legislation the system peak at that time that we're striving for was .5 percent. So, you know, we've made some strides there.

On Oahu approximately 10 percent of residential customers have installed PV systems on their home. No other State or utility is currently experiencing such high levels of customer sided PV. For this reason there's considerable interest in the next steps Hawaii will take as we continue to forge new ground.

With regard to financing.

It's a really exciting area for Hawaii. The Commission will self launch by summer its on bill program where electricity customers will be able to pay for efficiency or renewable improvements on their electricity bill through a tariff mechanism. The on bill program will have 2 components, an on bill financing mechanism where the public benefit fee will be leveraged for fixed efficiency improvements like solar water heaters and an on bill repayment mechanism where other entities may access the customer's electricity bill for repayment such as the Department of Business Economic Development and Tourism's Green Energy Market's Securitization or GEMS.

GEMS is a pioneering program which combines 2 tried and true financing methods, a traditional rate reduction bond structure and on bill financing in a synergistic model. This innovative structure can open the door for a whole new financing market in renewables and energy efficiency. So although the GEMS program was invented in Hawaii to serve Hawaii's residents and businesses the program has drawn national attention and could potentially serve as a model for other States.

DBEDT hopes to file its application for the GEMS program with the Commission to implement the program by this summer. The

Commission has just circulated its term sheet within the investment community and hope to get responses by the end of April for its efficiency program.

Just to sort of sum up our largest challenge in moving toward clean energy transformation.

I feel our biggest challenge and I think you've heard me mention this before, is moving from clean energy 1.0 to clean energy 2.0 and beyond. Clean energy 2.0 recognizes that transformation requires a systems approach requiring technology and economics to inform and shape policy, energy policy, to provide clean, safe, reliable, affordable electricity and achieve environmental and societal goals within a regulatory framework.

The second biggest challenge is the strategy and transition for a new electricity, electric utility business model and the regulatory reform necessary to facilitate this transition in a timely way, especially since we are so on the leading edge.

So recently my fellow Commissioner, Lorena Akiba remarked, Hawaii is a coast guard for the future. So while we're often cited for our success we are also trailblazers with big challenges before us.

So, thank you for this opportunity.

[The prepared statement of Ms. Morita follows:]

PREPARED STATEMENT OF HERMINA M. MORITA, CHAIR, HAWAII PUBLIC UTILITIES COMMISSION, HONOLULU, HI

Thank you for the opportunity to testify on Hawaii's success and its challenges in meeting its sustainability goals. Hawaii's Public Utilities Commission ("Commission") is responsible for the oversight of meeting Hawaii's clean energy statutes through its regulation of Hawaii's electric utilities and mandated programs. Today, I would like to share with the Committee (1) the key policy drivers under the jurisdiction of the Commission to accomplish Hawaii's clean energy transformation with an overview and status of each key policy driver; and (2) the challenges of accomplishing Hawaii's clean energy transformation.

Hawaii articulates a multi-prong approach in the implementation of Hawaii's clean energy future through the following laws:

- Renewable Energy Portfolio Standards ("RPS")
- Energy Efficiency Portfolio Standards ("EEPS")
- Public Benefit Fee ("PBF")
- Act 99, SLH 2012 ("Act 99")
    - —the public utilities commission shall consider the costs and benefits of a diverse fossil fuel portfolio and of maximizing the efficiency of all electric utility assets to lower and stabilize the cost of electricity

In its totality, Hawaii's energy policies attempt to shift the focus from individual renewable energy generation projects to a systems approach, requiring technology and economics to inform and shape energy decisions to advance three regulatory goals, while capturing environmental and social benefits:

1. Encourage prudent investments in and the utilization and optimization of all assets, both utility and non-utility, centralized and distributed, that bring efficient and cost-effective benefits and value to the electric system to serve the public good.

2. Appropriate allocation of fixed costs to maintain and enhance the electric system, i.e. a customer pays for the services received from the grid and is fairly compensated for services a customer provides to the grid.

3. Accessibility, fairness and the opportunity for all electricity customers to benefit from clean energy policies and programs.

KEY POLICY DRIVERS TO ENABLE HAWAII' S CLEAN ENERGY TRANSFORMATION

Renewable Portfolio Standard
    —10 percent of net electricity sales by December 31, 2010

—15 percent of net electricity sales by December 31, 2015
—25 percent of net electricity sales by December 31, 2020
—40 percent of net electricity sales by December 31, 2030

I am happy to report that Hawaiian Electric Company, and its subsidiaries, Hawaii Electric Light Company and Maui Electric Company (collectively the "HECO Companies"), have achieved a consolidated Renewable Portfolio Standard of 34.4 percent in 2013, which includes electrical savings from energy efficiency and solar water heating technologies.[1] This is an increase from the 28.7 percent achieved in 2012. Excluding electric energy savings, the renewable energy generation percentage for the HECO Companies is 18.2 percent.

The 2013 RPS report for Kauai Island Utility Cooperative ("KIUC") has not been filed with the Commission yet, however, KIUC increased its percentage from 14.69 in 2011 to 16.64 percent in 2012 and anticipates to have on-line by 2015 an additional 24 megawatts of utility scale photovoltaic and 6.7 megawatts of biomass.

Every five (5) years the Commission conducts a review of the RPS to ensure it is effective and achievable. Attached below is a link to the report:

Report to the 2014 Legislature on the Public Utilities Commission Review of Hawaii's Renewable Portfolio Standards—Issued Pursuant to Section 269-95(5), Hawaii Revised Statutes: http://puc.hawaii.gov/wp-content/uploads/2013/04/2013-PUC-RPS- Report___FINAL-w-Appnds.pdf

Several principal findings in this Report include:

- The 2015 RPS requirement of 15 percent is achievable for both the HECO Companies1 and Kauai Island Utility Cooperative ("KIUC").
- It appears likely that the 2020 RPS requirement of 25 percent is achievable for both the HECO Companies and KIUC, provided that reasonably expected amounts of currently proposed utility-scale renewable energy projects and distributed renewable generation are successfully developed and integrated on the utility systems.
- The 2030 RPS requirement of 40 percent may possibly be achievable, but this cannot be determined with confidence at this time due to uncertainties regarding the magnitude of future utility sales and several substantial outstanding challenges regarding the successful and economical siting and incorporation of requisite renewable energy generation resources. Nonetheless, this target is sufficiently aggressive to effectively focus efforts to address several challenges to the extensive incorporation of renewable resources on the Hawaii utility systems. A number of key issues must be thoughtfully considered when assessing whether current RPS targets should be adjusted or whether additional benchmarks should be established.
- The RPS remains effective in helping the State achieve its policies and objectives with respect to developing renewable energy resources in Hawaii through the 2030 timeframe.

The Commission anticipates that the results of pending investigations and reviews relevant to the RPS will further inform consideration of possible future amendments to the RPS targets.

Energy Efficiency Portfolio Standard

Hawaii's energy efficiency goals were enacted in 2009 and codified in Section 269-96, Hawaii Revised Statutes, establishing the EEPS at 4,300 gigawatt-hours ("GWh") of electricity saving by 2030.

Every five (5) years the Commission conducts a review of the EEPS. Attached below is a link to the report:

Report to the 2014 Legislature on Hawaii's Energy Efficiency Portfolio Standard—Issued Pursuant to Section 269-96, Hawaii Revised Statutes: http://puc.hawaii.gov/wp-   content/uploads/2013/04/2013-PUC-EEPS-Report___FINAL.pdf

Key findings of this Report include:

- The EEPS goals has proven effective at accelerating deployment of energy efficiency resources throughout the State. An estimated 794 GWh of electricity savings have been achieved statewide since the EEPS law took effect in 2009.
- While there is uncertainty about energy efficiency savings for future years, Hawaii is on track to achieve more than 1,550 GWh in savings by 2015, exceeding the interim 2015 EEPS target of 1,375 GWh by more than 12 percent.

---

[1] Beginning January 1, 2015, electrical savings shall not count toward renewable energy portfolio standards.

- Hawaii Energy, the ratepayer-funded energy efficiency services provider, is an essential component of the State's efforts to capture untapped energy efficiency resources, having contributed more than 80 percent of energy savings achieved since 2009.
- The long-term EEPS goal remains achievable. The cost-effective energy efficiency resource available statewide by 2030 exceeds the EEPS goal by nearly 50 percent. Energy efficiency remains a lower cost resource than most supply-side energy options, and provides many other important benefits to Hawaii's electricity utilities and ratepayers.

Public Benefit Fee

The Public Benefits Fee ("PBF") was enacted in 2009 and established in Section 269-121 through 125, Hawaii Revised Statutes, is collected by the HECO Companies from ratepayers through a demand-side management surcharge. The funds are used to support energy- efficiency programs and services, subject to the review and approval of the Commission. The law authorizes the Commission to contract with a third party administrator to implement and manage energy efficiency programs funded by the PBF. The program is called Hawaii Energy and administered by Leidos Engineering, LLC.

June 30, 2013 marked the completion of Hawaii Energy's fourth program year (the program year 2012 covered July 1, 2012 to June 30, 2013). The current surcharge amount is 1.5 percent of forecasted utility revenues, the PBF two-year budget for FY 2012 and FY 2013 was $71,103,608. The target for FY 2012 was $33,472,166. As detailed in Hawaii Energy's PY 2012 Annual Report, Hawaii Energy's programs for PY 2012 will deliver 1.4 billion kilowatt hours ("kWh") in lifetime savings at a total program cost of 2.3 cents per kWh (all in cost). This, in turn, will save an estimated equivalent of 2.4 million barrels of oil and 1.2 million tons to greenhouse gas emissions. At an average electricity price of 30.7 cents per kWh, customers will save approximately $405 million on their electricity bills over the life of the installed efficiency measures.

Hawaii Energy's programs are designed to evolve to enable Hawaii's clean energy transformation cost-effectively focused on the following:

- Legacy Demand Side Management Programs—modifying and upgrading programs to meet cost-effective tests
- Efficiency For All—ensuring all ratepayers benefit from the PBF including the underserved, neighbor islands and hard to reach customers like low-income ratepayers and renters
- Conservation—effecting behavioral changes, outreach and ally development
- Transformation—training and educational programs, developing energy leadership
- Sustainability—targeting indirect energy relationships like water-energy nexus

For additional information, the Hawaii Energy Annual Report can be found at the following address: http://puc.hawaii.gov/wp-content/uploads/2013/04/HawaiiEnergyPY2012AnnualPlan7.19.2012.pdf

Act 99, 2012 Session Laws of Hawaii

More than half of an electricity customer's bill is comprised of fuel and purchased power cost. Through Act 99, the Legislature mandated the public utilities commission to consider the costs and benefits of a diverse fossil fuel portfolio and of maximizing the efficiency of all electric utility assets to lower and stabilize the cost of electricity. Currently, Hawaii's electricity and gas utilities are carefully examining the feasibility and cost benefit analysis to consider the importation of liquefied natural gas to help reduce the cost of fuel and improve air quality as well as the choice of fuel to enable more flexible generators to increase the penetration of variable renewable resources such as wind and solar.

As a regulator and as a community, one of the challenges of effecting a clean energy transformation is moving the discussion and focus off of Clean Energy 1.0 to Clean Energy 2.0. In Clean Energy 1.0, our energy policies were based on rewarding early adoption of renewable energy technologies. Clean Energy 1.0 is simple to understand, quantify, discuss and promote. These policies, such as net metering and the renewable energy income tax credit, were primarily focused on the cost of a renewable project. However, as technologies advance and cost are driven down, these policies have distorted the market where we are now faced with some perverse effects on the ratepayer who is unable to afford or cannot participate in these renewable programs. Unfortunately, these type of political policies are not structured to react quickly to fix these market distortions.

Clean Energy 2.0 recognizes that transformation requires a systems approach, requiring technology and economics to inform and shape desired energy outcomes.

Hawaii's electric grids represent the critical energy infrastructure that is required to advance to and beyond Clean Energy 2.0 and to serve the public good.

—The grid provides essential system support services for all customers to enable electricity to be used efficiently, reliably and safely and, desirably, at affordable rates.

—The grid is required also integrate clean, lower-cost, renewable energy from large scale, centralized solar and wind plants.

—The grid is also required in order to accept excess generation from customer-sited distributed PV used to offset energy usage (e.g., the NEM program) as well as provide the services required to ensure reliability when there is no generation or inadequate generation from those sites.

However, the existing grid infrastructure was not designed to accommodate large amounts of distributed, variable generation that is being rapidly added to each island system due to customer demand and technological improvements that have significantly reduced the cost of these alternative customer options.

It is viewed that the future of Hawaii's electric grids will be integrated systems with diversified portfolios of modern, quick-starting, flexible, and efficient generation combined with substantial amounts of lower-cost renewable generation (both centralized and distributed), as well as new technologies such as demand response and energy storage to provide the necessary grid services to ensure reliable power.

Modernizing Hawaii's island grids is a fundamental responsibility of the electric utilities and a prerequisite for meeting customer demands and the state's clean energy goals. This leads me into the second challenge of Hawaii's clean energy transformation which, I believe, can only be acted upon by the utility, that is, the electric utility as the system integrator. As the system integrator, the utility would be agnostic and price sensitive in utilizing a diverse portfolio of resources and technologies in optimizing the system to achieve an affordable, safe, reliable and sustainable energy services not only to support the electric system, but also our economic objectives and environmental values.

With emerging smart technologies and its corresponding data management and analytics, forwarding thinking utility executives, like many of their counterparts in other sectors are becoming increasingly aware of and taking advantage of big data as the next frontier for innovation, competition and increased productivity. Progressive electric utility executives understand the paradigm shift smart technologies brings to the generation, overall operations and distribution of electricity, as well as how it will redefine a utility's relationship with its customers and other service providers to the electric system. How timely a utility can process, analyze, synthesize and effectively use the information it gathers will require a huge cultural change within the utility, between and within silo'ed functions, to accommodate a data driven utility. Without this deep organizational cultural change, I am afraid Hawaii's clean energy transformation will be difficult to realize. The need to take a systems approach and how quickly and effectively utility can gather, analyze, synthesize and use the information in the management of the electric system are key drivers to effectuate Hawaii's clean energy transformation and the key to all this is the ability to optimize the productivity of an intelligent electrical grid.

Senator SCHATZ. Thank you very much.

Ms. Lippert.

STATEMENT OF DAWN LIPPERT, DIRECTOR, ENERGY EXCELERATOR, (a program of PICHTR), HONOLULU, HI

Ms. LIPPERT. Aloha and thank you to Senator Schatz and this committee for the invitation to testify today.

I'd actually like to take this opportunity to speak about the Energy Excelerator and what, I believe, it has taught us about the role of public/private partnerships in accelerating innovation.

The Energy Excelerator is a program of PICHTR and startup program designed to help energy innovation companies succeed starting in Hawaii.

Why starting in Hawaii?

The Senator knows the answer to this question. But 7 years ago I was fortunate enough to join the analysis team drafting the Hawaii Clean Energy Initiative which we've spoken about today. It is bold initiative to set the stage for energy transformation in Hawaii from an economy 90 percent dependent on oil to one powered by 70 percent clean, local energy.

At the time it would have been impossible to predict how powerful that was and the accelerated moment that this State has seen toward clean energy and the role we played as a model for other parts of the world. By many standards we are making great strides toward that goal. As Mina said, solar, for example, has increased 60 fold over the last few years. Eleven percent of Oahu households now have solar.

This success has also led to challenges. It's not easy to integrate all of these new renewables onto our island grids. We now know that we actually can't reach the 70 percent clean energy goal unless we adopt new technologies and develop new approaches.

This is where entrepreneurship becomes linked with the future of Hawaii and where I believe the Energy Excelerator comes in. Hawaii is now a fertile place for energy entrepreneurs. Entrepreneurs like to go to where the pain is highest and the urgency is most immediate.

To energy entrepreneurs Hawaii and other island nations are not seen as vacation destinations, but rather lands of opportunity.

Our Energy Excelerator has capitalized on this opportunity to launch a unique program that was designed based on interviews with entrepreneurs. We asked them what they really needed to move their technology from the lab to the market. Our new model borrows the best from tech accelerators like Y Combinator which are designed for web and mobile technologies and the traditional grant process organizations like the Department of Energy to create the combined structure of Energy Excelerator.

What are the best of each of these that we've picked?

We've adopted the cohort aspect of Y Combinator with a major focus on peer to peer learning and from the Department of Energy we emulate significant technology funding of up to $1 million needed to support technology commercialization along with an insistence on customer development and business models.

A vibrant ecosystem is needed to sustain these business relationships. Our companies work and grow together and even stay together in one house in a kind of real world clean tech. It's created a family style community of clean energy startups. If you talk to any of our entrepreneurs they'll tell you that this feeling of Ohana is something that sets us apart.

But there's one other thing that makes us different. We call it place centered innovation. We don't just pick the 15 hottest energy companies each year. We pick the 15 most likely to transform the Hawaii energy system to help us integrate the next trench of solar, to fill gaps in our transportation system, to make buildings smarter and more efficient.

This is really a systems approach to innovation. It is starting in Hawaii. But we believe it can be applied throughout the Nation and around the world in outreach and partnerships.

So the question is does this work?

Can we do 2 things at once?

Immediately impact the success of clean energy startups and also transform the Hawaii energy system through place centered innovation?

The jury is, frankly, still out. But early metrics are positive. Our companies have raised $55 million in follow on funding and created over 400 jobs.

Over 1,000 startups have expressed interest in this program putting Hawaii on the map for investors and entrepreneurs around the world. So far we have raised nearly $35 million in public and private funding from for the Energy Excelerator from organizations such as the Department of Defense, Office of Naval Research, the Department of Energy, Hawaiian Electric Industries and others. We are just getting started.

But time will tell this vision requires long term investment and commitment.

While over 1,000 energy startups have expressed interest in the Energy Excelerator we have funded just 32. It is important to recognize that these companies come not just with ideas but often with millions of dollars of grant funding already invested in research. The government has invested significant resources in research and development for important technologies that have not yet made it to market.

We designed Energy Excelerator specifically to get these companies across the gap that exists between the lab and commercial sales. We iterate and evolve our program continuously to better achieve this goal.

Based on my personal experience in the Hawaiian Clean Energy Initiative and the Energy Excelerator innovative public/private partnerships like ours, can be major catalysts to deploying sustainable clean energy technology while also playing a major role in addressing local challenges and creating a vibrant economy in the process. For all of here one of the deeply important elements of achieving our clean energy goals is the opportunity to create high quality jobs in a knowledge based economy, the types of jobs that our children will aspire to.

I was encouraged to see the interns here today. I'm also happy to announce that we're launching an internship program with our companies to put interns in all of our clean energy startups. I think this is a really important piece of developing the next generation clean energy task force that can work productively with emerging technology.

Finally, on a personal note I just want to say this has not been an easy road. We are embarking on a journey that is ambitious, risky and highly entrepreneurial.

I'd also like to sincerely thank Senator Schatz and his staff, our Congressional delegation, this committee, our public and private partners and others in the community who have believed in this vision and help make it possible.

Thank you.

[The prepared statement of Ms. Lippert follows:]

PREPARED STATEMENT OF DAWN LIPPERT, DIRECTOR, ENERGY EXCELERATOR (A
PROGRAM OF PICHTR), HONOLULU, HI

Aloha and thank you to Senator Schatz and this committee for the invitation to
testify today. I'd like to take this opportunity to speak about the Energy Excelerator
and what I believe it has taught us about the role of public-private partnerships in
accelerating innovation.

Innovation in a Hawaii Context

The Energy Excelerator, a program of Pacific International Center for High Technology Research, is a startup program designed to help energy innovation companies
succeed, starting in Hawaii. Why starting in Hawaii? Seven years ago I was fortunate to join the analysis team drafting the Hawaii Clean Energy Initiative. It is a
bold initiative to set the stage for energy transformation in Hawaii—from an economy 90 percent dependent on oil to one powered by 70 percent clean, local energy.
At the time, it would have been impossible to predict how powerful that was, and
the accelerated momentum this state has seen toward clean energy and the role
we've played as a model for other parts of the world. By many standards, we are
making great strides toward that goal. Solar, for example, has increased 60-fold over
the last few years. Eleven percent of Oahu households now have solar. This success
has also led to challenges—it's not easy to integrate all of these new renewables
onto our island grids. We now know that we actually can't reach the 70 percent
clean energy goal unless we adopt new technologies and develop new approaches.
This is where entrepreneurship becomes linked with the future of Hawaii—and
where the Energy Excelerator comes in. Hawaii is now a fertile place for energy entrepreneurs; entrepreneurs like to go where the pain is highest and the urgency is
most immediate. To energy entrepreneurs, Hawaii and other island nations are not
seen as vacation destinations, but rather lands of opportunity.

Place-based Innovation

Our Energy Excelerator organization has capitalized on this opportunity to launch
a unique program that was designed based on interviews with entrepreneurs. We
asked them what they really needed to move their technology from the lab to the
market. Our new model borrows the best from tech accelerators like YCombinator,
designed for web and mobile, and the traditional grant process of organizations like
Department of Energy, to create the Energy Excelerator. What are the best of each
that we've picked? We have adopted the cohort aspect of YCombinator, with a major
focus on peer-to-peer learning, and from the Department of Energy, we emulate significant technology funding of up to $1 million needed to support commercialization,
along with an insistence on customer development. A vibrant ecosystem is needed
to sustain these business relationships. Our companies work and grow together, and
even stay together in a kind of Real-World-Cleantech. It's created a family-style
community of clean energy startups, and if you talk to any of our entrepreneurs,
they'll tell you that this is something that sets us apart.

But there is one other thing that makes us different. We call it "place-centered
innovation." We don't just pick the 15 hottest energy companies each year. We pick
the 15 most likely to transform the Hawaii energy system—to help us integrate the
next tranche of solar, to fill gaps in our transportation system, to make buildings
smarter and more efficient. This is a systems approach to innovation. It is starting
in Hawaii but we believe it can be applied throughout the nation and around the
world with outreach and partnerships.

How it's Worked So Far—Results

So the question is—does this work? Can we do two things at once: 1) meaningfully
impact the success of clean energy startups and, 2) also transform the Hawaii energy system through "place-centered innovation"? Early metrics are positive; our
companies have raised $55 million in follow-on funding and created over 400 jobs.
Over 1000 startups have expressed interest in the program, putting Hawaii on the
map for entrepreneurs and investors around the world. So far we have raised nearly
$35 million in public and private funding for the Energy Excelerator—from organi-
zations such the Department of Defense's Office of Naval Research, the Department
of Energy, Hawaiian Electric Industries, and others, and we're just getting started.
But time will tell; this vision requires long-term investment and commitment.

While over 1000 energy startups have expressed interest in the Energy
Excelerator, we have funded 32. It is important to recognize that these companies
come with not just ideas, but often with millions of dollars of grant funding already
invested in research. The government has invested significant resources in research
and development for important technologies that have not yet made it to market.
We designed the Energy Excelerator specifically to get these companies across the

gap that exists between the lab and commercial sales. We iterate and evolve our program continuously to better achieve this goal.

Based on my experience in the Hawaii Clean Energy Initiative and the Energy Excelerator, innovative public-private partnerships like ours can be major catalysts to deploying sustainable energy technology, while also playing a major role in addressing local challenges—and creating a vibrant economy in the process. For all of us here, one of the deeply important elements of achieving our clean energy goals is the opportunity to create high quality jobs in a knowledge-based economy—the types of jobs that our children will aspire to.

In Closing

On a personal note, I want to say that this has not been an easy road; we are embarking on a journey that is ambitious, risky, and highly entrepreneurial. And I would like to sincerely thank Senator Schatz and his staff, our Congressional delegation, this committee, our public and private partners, and others in the community who have believed in this vision and helped make it possible. Mahalo.

Senator SCHATZ. Thank you very much.

Ms. Meguro.

STATEMENT OF WENDY MEGURO, ASSISTANT PROFESSOR, SUSTAINABLE BUILDINGS AND COMMUNITY DESIGN, UNIVERSITY OF HAWAII, MANOA, SCHOOL OF ARCHITECTURE AND SEA GRANT COLLEGE PROGRAM, HONOLULU, HI

Ms. MEGURO. First I would like to thank you for this invitation to speak about sustainability challenges and opportunities in Hawaii and also to summarize some of the themes from our ASCENT conference yesterday.

The overarching message that you mentioned in your introduction that I heard yesterday was that we have the knowledge. We have the technology to live sustainably here in Hawaii. Now we need the political will.

As Vice President Al Gore said yesterday, political will is a renewable resource. So Senator Schatz, the people of Hawaii trust you to be the steward of that political will.

The subject that I would like to focus on is green buildings, specifically managing the energy water nexus in the built environment.

Here in Hawaii where our environment is our economy, buildings use over 25 percent of our energy. In addition the energy water nexus illustrates that the energy is used to transport and treat water and water is used in power plants to create our electricity.

For example, the Board of Water Supply is one of Hawaiian electric company's largest customers.

There are many aspects to green buildings but we chose to focus on efficiency in our session yesterday. Improving energy and water efficiency in buildings is one of the easiest and most cost effective ways to mitigate climate change to improve our local air and water quality and to reduce utility costs for consumers.

So why focus on efficiency?

It's estimated that a dollar spent on development of technology that improves the efficiency of building infrastructure is considerably worth $3 to $4 worth—spent on renewable energy technology.

One successful example which has been cited multiple times today of Federal, State and private collaboration to address energy efficiency in buildings is the Hawaii Clean Energy Initiative.

So I applaud the efforts so far. I also wanted to point out I think it's particularly useful because of its quantitative energy reduction targets and also specific recommended strategies. So I would like to emphasize those as we move into the future.

I think we should continue to monitor our progress and communicate our updated recommendations for building energy efficiency to the public.

In addition we should continue to foster advancements in energy saving building technologies and practices on the horizon.

Next, I would like to discuss how policymakers might address some challenges and opportunities to reduce energy use in buildings.

First, Hawaii's building energy and water codes are outdated. There's an opportunity to push for the adoption of current building energy and water codes by all counties. This also happens to align the HCEI recommendations. In parallel training on the new codes should be provided for building code inspectors and design professionals.

Second, in Hawaii green building incentives do not yet reflect the caliber of a building's environmental benefit. Consider creating incentives for green building projects which are ratcheted to reward exemplary performance, particularly in water and energy savings. In addition, consider giving awards to recognize exceptionally high performance buildings and developments.

Third, yesterday we talked in the opening session about acceptable return on investments. The question came up the ROI of what? What are we measuring?

Higher first costs can discourage building owners from implementing energy efficient practices or technologies. We need to have adequate construction budgets or without that, provide financial incentives to offset those higher first costs. The goal is to be able to recognize and assess the quantity of value associated with water and greenhouse gas emission savings, reduce demands on municipal infrastructure and improved occupant health.

In a commercial building the ratio of first cost to operating cost to personnel cost is about 1 to 5 to 200. So this highlights the economic benefit that green buildings provide occupants in terms of day lighting, high indoor air quality, control over one's comfort.

Moving on to the subject of water and buildings.

Challenges in Hawaii include maintaining our sustainable water supply and also reducing greenhouse gas emissions from water transport and treatment. Moderate water savings have been achieved already which, I applaud, using green building rating systems for both fleet buildings and for schools.

I think this is a great start. But Hawaii has not yet seized the opportunity to save water and energy by capturing and using non potable water, onsite, in large scale buildings. Potable water is defined as suitable for human consumption and we typically do not need potable water to flush our toilets, to irrigate and to send to our cooling towers. So there's an opportunity here to match water quality with its appropriate use.

We have multiple sources of water in a building which can be captured, treated and used onsite including green water, grey water, black water, cooling tower blow down, air conditioning condensate, etcetera. Multiple of our Hawaii based plans already encourage Hawaii or Hawaii to recycle and use non potable water including the Hawaii 2050 Sustainability Plan, the Hawaii Green Business Guide and the Hawaii Water Conservation Plan. So why aren't we on board yet or why don't we have these big projects yet?

I would suggest that you consider initiating pilot projects with onsite water treatment and non potable water use in a large scale building or district. Relevant stakeholders to include in the conversation include the State Building Code Council, the Public Utilities Commission, the Board of Water Supply, the Department of Health, Worker's Unions and individuals who have already been involved in our non potable water workshops series. Pilot projects would establish a processes for permitting and inspection as well as training for code officials, designers and laborers.

In addition, consider a study to quantify the potential energy and economic benefits of distributive water treatments verses the traditional centralized municipal water system. This might be timely considering the upcoming municipal water treatment plant upgrades that are required by the EPA.

I appreciate your time and look forward to discussion.

[The prepared statement of Ms. Meguro follows:]

PREPARED STATEMENT OF WENDY MEGURO, ASSISTANT PROFESSOR, SUSTAINABLE BUILDINGS AND COMMUNITY DESIGN, UNIVERSITY OF HAWAII, MANOA, SCHOOL OF ARCHITECTURE AND SEA GRANT COLLEGE PROGRAM, HONOLULU, HI

I would like to thank you for the invitation to speak about sustainability challenges and opportunities in Hawai'i, and to summarize themes from the Ascent conference on April 15th.

The subject I would like to focus on is "green buildings," specifically, managing the energy-water nexus in the built environment. Here in Hawai'i, where the environment is the economy, buildings use over 25 percent of our energy. (Energy Information Administration) Most of that energy generation relies on imported fossil fuels and contributes to climate change. In addition, the energy-water nexus illustrates that energy is used to transport and treat water, and water is used in power plants to create energy. The Board of Water Supply is one of Hawaiian Electric Company's largest customers.

Improving energy and water efficiency in buildings is one of the easiest and most cost effective ways to mitigate climate change, improve our local air and water quality, and reduce utility costs for consumers. Why focus on efficiency? It is estimated that $1 spent on the development of technology that improves the efficiency of building and transportation infrastructure is conservatively worth $3-4 (likely as high as $8-10) spent on renewable energy technology (Lawrence Berkeley National Laboratory).

A successful example of a federal, state, and private collaboration to address energy efficiency in buildings is the Hawai'i Clean Energy Initiative (HCEI). One of its goals is to reduce energy use by 30 percent by 2030 through efficiency and conservation (not including renewable energy). HCEI is especially useful because it has quantitative energy reduction targets and specific recommended strategies. We should continue to monitor our progress and communicate updated recommendations to the public. In addition, we should continue to foster advancements in energy-saving building technologies and practices.

Next, I would like to discuss how policy-makers may address some challenges and opportunities to reduce energy use in buildings.

First, Hawai'i's building energy codes are outdated. There is an opportunity to push for the adoption of current building energy codes by all counties. This also happens to align with HCEI recommendations. In parallel, training on the new codes should be provided for building code inspectors and design professionals.

Second, in Hawai'i, green building incentives do not reflect the caliber of the building's environmental benefit. Consider creating incentives for green building projects which are ratcheted to reward exemplary performance, particularly in water and energy savings.

Third, higher first costs can discourage building owners from implementing energy efficient practices and technologies. We need to have adequate construction budgets or provide financial incentives to offset higher first costs. The goal is to recognize and value the associated water and greenhouse gas emissions savings, reduced demands on municipal infrastructure, and improved occupant health. In a commercial building, the ratio of first costs to operating costs to personnel costs is about 1: 5: 200. (The Long Term Costs of Owning and Using Buildings, The Royal Academy of Engineering) This highlights the economic benefit of high performance buildings that provide occupants with daylight, high indoor air quality, and control over one's comfort.

On the subject of water and buildings, challenges in Hawai'i include maintaining a sustainable water supply and reducing the greenhouse gas emissions from water transport and treatment. Moderate water savings have been achieved by using green building rating systems in State buildings and schools. (Lead by Example and Collaborative for High Performance Schools)

This is a good start, but Hawai'i has not yet seized the opportunity to save water and energy by capturing and using non-potable water on-site in large scale buildings. Potable water is defined as suitable for human consumption, and we typically do not need potable water to flush our toilets, irrigate, or use in cooling towers. There is an opportunity is to match water quality and its appropriate use.

A building has multiple water resources which can be captured, treated, and used, including rainwater; greywater from sinks, showers, laundry; blackwater from water closets; cooling tower blow down; air conditioning condensate; pool filter back flush; and more. Multiple Hawai'i-based plans encourage water recycling or non-potable water use, including the Hawai'i 2050 Sustainability Plan, the Hawai'i Green Business Guide, and the Hawai'i Water Conservation Plan.

Consider initiating pilot projects with on-site water treatment and non-potable water use in a large-scale building or district. Relevant stakeholders include the State Building Code Council, the Board of Water Supply, and the Department of Health, workers unions, and individuals involved in the existing non-potable water workshop series. Pilot projects would establish processes for permitting and inspection as well as training for code officials, designers and laborers. In addition, a study is recommended to quantify the potential energy and economic benefits of distributed water treatment versus the traditional municipal water system. It is timely considering upcoming municipal water treatment plant upgrades are required by the EPA.

I appreciate your time and welcome discussion.

Senator SCHATZ. Thank you very much.

Mr. Rue.

STATEMENT OF HARRISON RUE, COMMUNITY BUILDING AND TOD ADMINISTRATOR, CITY AND COUNTY OF HOLOLULU, DEPARTMENT OF PLANNING AND PERMITTING, HONOLULU, HI

Mr. RUE. Senator Schatz, thank you so much for the opportunity to testify today. But first I do have to say how delighted I was to hear the testimony of the gentleman from Roosevelt. My son graduated Roosevelt a dozen years ago and go, Rough Riders. That's all I have to say.

[Laughter.]

Mr. RUE. Great testimony.

I'd like to talk about the City and County of Honolulu's Community Building and Transit-Oriented Development program and offer some suggestions on what Federal agencies and Congress can do to support local actions in sustainable community design or transportation. These also highlight some of the discussions in our community design panel at yesterday's ASCENT conference.

I would like to also to thank you for your support for the conference and for your—yesterday.

The TOD program is a community based program planning effort to help revitalize neighborhoods, increase transportation and housing choices and create more livable neighborhoods around the city's 20 mile rail transit system now under construction. We've developed neighborhood TOD plans for two-thirds of the 21 stations so far. We're updating land use ordinances and overlay zoning to require operable mixed use development.

While we have big plans, policies and projects, we need to remember this is really about people and their neighborhoods and how we can connect families with jobs, housing, gathering spaces and each other. It's not an infrastructure project.

The city's new TOD subcabinet is a working group of department directors modeled on the HUD, DOT, EPA Sustainable Communities Partnership. We meet weekly to identify and solve obstacles, address feasibility infrastructure availability, coordinate strategies and budgets and act together on collaborative projects. The TOD team works effectively with outside partners including several State agencies, land owners and developers and non profits and allied organizations.

Other work underway include a proposed bike share system to reduce parking standards, new complete street standards, protected bike lanes and updated housing strategy and a TOD financial tool kit. This work will increase transportation choice access and safety, reduce energy use and emissions, by the way, that may be some of the missing things that are not in the HTI plan, a good percentage can come in there, folks, help protect water resources through compact development and green infrastructure and improve human and environmental health.

To support these ongoing activities and partnerships we suggest that the Federal Government consider the following options most of which can be done with an existing authority and not asking for new money.

We suggest replicating and expanding the successful interagency coordination programs like the HUD, DOT, EPA, Sustainable Communities Partnership. This is an excellent combination of funding, technical assistance that encourages innovation, collaboration and performance monitoring.

I was just talking with one of the former directors yesterday who was at the conference. She noted that it has touched one third of the U.S. population in various programs.

There's a strong need for continued technical assistance to the hundreds of existing grantees, expanded guidance and training materials based on lessons learned and most importantly corporation partnerships, principles and collaborative approach in the conventional statutory funding and regulatory programs.

We also suggest that expanding this interagency approach to address broader issues using a variety of funding streams across other different agencies. One way to consider, you know, streamlined performance would be to use, it sounds simple, but just using the reporting and public involvement requirements for the single, cognizant agency much like when we received Federal grants. Only one cognizant agency is bonded to those grants. So you could actually rather than have 4 different agencies, environmental justice and public participation requirements just follow one of them.

We suggest rewarding local efforts to strengthen interagency coordination and targeted budgeting for our areas much like the Federal partnership. The—our TOD subcabinet, that I noted, has the records of all relevant departments meeting weekly to coordinate, and prioritize projects and move them forward. Suggest maybe making such local coordination a consideration for demonstrating potential for follow through and grant making.

We're also suggesting leveraging existing and future funding toward more integrated resilience efforts. Statutory programs tend to produce the same kinds of projects each year. Reallocating a larger percentage of existing, available funding toward innovative, local projects, such as DOD Tiger grant program, would require proof that investments will cost effectively meet multimodal, environmental and safety performance codes.

We also suggest adjusting the MAP 21 rules in future reauthorization legislation to require a more sustainable performance measures that address broader community goals and link land use, community design, health, safety, equity and environmental sustainability.

Not only do we encourage agencies like EPA to continue stepping out of their regulatory framework to work cooperatively with local and State governments to develop more cost effective, long term solutions to rain water and waste water issues.

Green infrastructure can do an equal or better job of protecting watersheds while supporting other sustainability goals like compact development, transportation, housing choice to reduce energy use.

Thank you again for the opportunity to testify. We appreciate the committee's willingness to conduct this hearing and to work on these critical issues.

[The prepared statement of Mr. Rue follows:]

PREPARED STATEMENT OF HARRISON RUE, COMMUNITY BUILDING AND TOD ADMINISTRATOR, CITY AND COUNTY OF HONOLULU, DEPARTMENT OF PLANNING AND PERMITTING, HONOLULU, HI

Thank you so much for the opportunity to testify today. In addition to briefly summarizing the City and County of Honolulu's Transit Oriented Development Program, my testimony will focus on what federal agencies and Congress can do to support state and local actions in sustainable community design and transportation initiatives.

The City and County of Honolulu's TOD Program is a community-based planning effort to help revitalize neighborhoods, increase transportation and housing choices, and create more livable communities around the City's 21 rapid transit rail stations. After four decades of heated discussion, public opinion, political support, and financial capacity have aligned to begin construction of The Honolulu Rail Transit Project, a 20-mile high capacity transit system that will connect families with jobs, housing, gathering spaces, and each other. Together with public and private partners, the TOD Program is turning the focus toward using the transit investment to enhance and revitalize neighborhoods. The TOD team has developed Neighborhood TOD Plans for 2/3 of the 21 stations, with the remainder under way. The City is updating land use ordinances and developing overlay zoning to encourage walkable, mixed-use development.

Our implementation strategy is intended to catalyze development opportunities, infrastructure investments, and neighborhood enhancements around the rail stations. The City's new TOD Sub-cabinet is a working group of infrastructure, transportation, environmental, housing, and planning directors who meet weekly to focus inter-agency efforts on expediting catalytic projects in the TOD areas, with a focus on feasibility, infrastructure availability, market interest, and ability to leverage other investments. This approach is modeled on the success of the HUD-DOT-EPA Sustainable Communities Partnership. The subcabinet meets weekly to identify and solve obstacles, facilitate development, coordinate strategies and budgets, and act together on catalytic projects. The TOD team also works effectively with outside partners including state and federal agencies, landowners and developers, and non-profits and allied organizations including union and construction industry partnerships.

Related efforts include a proposed bikeshare system, reduced parking standards, new complete streets polices and standards, protected bike lanes, and a TOD financial toolkit. Together, these plans, policies, and projects will increase transportation choice, access, and safety; reduce energy use and emissions; help protect water resources through compact development and green infrastructure; connect people with jobs and businesses with customers; and improve human and environmental health.

We have been working with several State agencies on TOD-related issues, including the Department of Education (potential redevelopment opportunities and school access); Department of Health (potential bike share system and environmental/ brownfields issues); Department of Accounting and General Services (potential State facilities and projects in TOD areas); Department of Planning (TOD planning and policy); Department of Hawaiian Home Lands (East Kapolei, Kalihi and downtown TOD plans); HCDA (Downtown and East Kapolei Plans, and mobility and infrastructure improvements in Kakaako); HHFDC (housing policy and project finance); Hawaii Public Housing Authority (Kalihi and Downtown TOD plans); DLNR (development of the East Kapolei TOD Plan); and the University of Hawaii system (West Oahu, Leeward Community College, and Honolulu Community College campuses and long-term redevelopment potential). We have initiated the Airport Neighborhood TOD Plan, and will be working closely with the Hawaii Department of Transportation on that plan, as well as transit station access and safety improvements for the station areas along Farrington and Kamehameha highways.

To support these ongoing activities and partnerships, we suggest that the federal government consider the following options:

- Replicate and expand successful interagency coordination programs like the HUD-DOT-EPA Sustainable Communities Partnership. These have worked exceptionally well to encourage innovation at the local and state level. They are an excellent combination of funding and technical assistance that encourages innovation, collaboration and performance monitoring. These included HUD's regional planning and community challenge grants (which Honolulu received), DOT's TIGER grants, and EPA's robust technical assistance and research. Many of these included adaptation and resilience strategies for transportation, water, energy and infrastructure. There is a strong need for 1) continued technical assistance to the hundreds of existing grantees; 2) expanded guidance and training materials for other interested local government partnerships based on lessons learned to date; and 3) incorporation of the Partnership's principles and collaborative approach into conventional and statutory funding and regulatory programs.

- This interagency approach could be expanded on to encourage more integrated resilience strategies that address multiple infrastructure issues and utilize a variety of funding streams across different agencies. While it can be more difficult to 'complicate' grant-making and reporting this way, the government should consider ways to streamline grantmaking and reporting when coordinating funding awards, such as using the reporting and public involvement requirements of a single cognizant agency (much like the approach to using a single cognizant agency's requirements in auditing funding).

- Encourage local efforts to develop more integrated resilience solutions by rewarding local and state efforts to strengthen interagency coordination and targeted budgeting priorities, much like the HUD-DOT-EPA Partnership. One example of this is the City and County of Honolulu's TOD Sub-cabinet, which has directors of all infrastructure, planning, environmental, transportation, economic development, operations, and housing departments meet weekly to coordinate and prioritize projects in neighborhoods along the city's 20-mile rail transit project (now under construction). Such local coordination could potentially be a consideration for demonstrating potential for follow-through in grantmaking.

- Provide more opportunities to leverage existing funding toward integrated resilience efforts (in addition to developing new funding streams). Much of the existing funding in transportation, housing, water, energy, and environmental programs is statutory in nature, and goes through older programs and existing agency structures at federal, state, and local levels. Re-allocating a larger percentage of available funding toward more innovative programs that can go directly to local integrated projects, such as DOT's TIGER grant program, would help advance and prove the results of innovation. Statutory formula funds tend to produce the same kinds of projects each year; innovation-driven programs like TIGER require proof that investments will cost-effectively meet multimodal, environmental, and safety performance goals.

- Adjust the MAP-21 rules and future Reauthorization legislation to encourage/require performance measures that address broader community goals that link land use, community design, health, safety, equity, and environmental sustainability.
- Encourage agencies like EPA to step out of their regulatory framework to work cooperatively with local and state governments to develop more cost-effective long-term solutions to stormwater issues that do an equal or better job of protecting watersheds, while supporting other sustainability goals like compact development, transportation and housing choice, and reduced energy use. Include training, technical assistance and funding support for revising local and state codes and standards to allow/encourage/require green infrastructure and resilience solutions.

Thank you again for the opportunity to testify; we appreciate the committee's willingness to conduct this field hearing and to work on these critical issues.

Senator SCHATZ. Thank you, Mr. Rue.

Mr. Tam.

STATEMENT OF WILLIAM M. TAM, DEPUTY DIRECTOR, HAWAII COMMISSION ON WATER RESOURCE MANAGEMENT (CWRM), DEPARTMENT OF LAND AND NATURAL RESOURCES (DLNR), HONOLULU, HI

Mr. TAM. Thank you, Senator Schatz.

First we'd like to thank you for your introduction of the Secure Water Act of 2014 which will allow the State of Hawaii to compete for grants, water smart grants, water efficiency, water optimization, VUE grants and advance water treatment demonstration projects. We think this is an important addition to our ability to be nubile in the future.

We'd also encourage you to pay attention to the decline in the number of stream gauges and the monitoring wells which are important in Hawaii. Both have suffered from lack of funding. We think these are critical. If you are a patient that's concerned about being healthy you do not want to take the monitor away when you most need it.

In Hawaii all the water is local. Water and energy have a very interesting combination, but they move in different ways. Water is heavier, obviously. It can't be moved around in the same way energy can be. So it's important to look at the cost effects of that as we go forward.

The World Economic Global Risks 2014 identified water prices and the failure of climate change. Mitigation adaptation is the third and fifth, respectively in its ranking order of the 10 global risks of highest concern in 2014. They considered these risks to have a high likelihood and a high impact, unlike the proverbial black swan which has low probability, but high impact. The climate change issues coming before us are both high impact and high probability.

So this is a gale force wind that is coming toward us. As Nainoa Thompson reminded us yesterday, you're building a canoe to sail around the world you don't plan for the sunny afternoon offshore, you plan for the gale force winds and the low tide channels in 15 foot seas at night. So the question is is the—are the lashings correctly done. Is the crew ready? Because when a voyage goes around the world, one bad night and the voyage is over.

So as we design our climate change adaptation and resilience, we need to take into account that that's what we have to look for.

Economics is very important. I'm going to talk about that in just a moment. The goal of the journey is to get there. It's not to do an accounting, necessarily, where we meet and auditors report, although those things have their place.

So when we think about these issues we could do something that's cheap. But I think what we have to look at is what is the black swan of a major event? What happens if Fukushima earthquakes 1,000 miles South comes at us from the Southwest on Oahu, hits the—power plant, takes out—and Honolulu. It takes out Sand Island wastewater treatment plant. The harbors and our airports are hit.

What do you do to build a future when that is a possibility? There's a huge earthquake. The Pacific is a rich area in seismic events. We need to think about how to build those resiliencies into our system which suggests that local, distributed and simple—systems that are in a community and that's a new way of doing things.

With the model we've built from the 50s and 60s was good for that time. But we're now faced with a different set of circumstances. So we need to think about how to build resistance and duplication into our systems.

To give you a simple example of what Hermina eluded to earlier about the cost of water and what some of the savings might be. Rural water supply was an issue yesterday spends about $28 million, $26 million for 87 million kilowatt/hours pumping 43 million gallons a day which is about $187,500 to pump 1 million gallons for a year. That's on the front side of the water cycle.

On the back side of the water cycle environmental services pumps—or costs about—spends about $24 million to pump 74 million, I'm sorry. It used to be 74 million kilowatt/hours for about 100 million gallons. That's about $244,000 a year to pump 1 million gallons of sewage.

So combined the electrical costs alone to move a million gallons of water is $431,500 a year. That's not including—on top of expenses or disrupted—of electricity.

You can buy down a million gallons per day of water savings through conservation activities in the agricultural areas and the other areas. So that's where—that's a line we can start to look at.

Senator SCHATZ. You said $430 odd thousand a year per million?

Mr. TAM. Per million gallons of water.

Senator SCHATZ. How many gallons are we moving?

Mr. TAM. That's the average for one million gallons to be pumped out of the ground, transferred to your home, transferred to the wastewater treatment facility and then moved 2 miles offshore off Sand Island or Honolulu.

Senator SCHATZ. Wait. But how many gallons are we moving on Oahu annually?

Mr. TAM. Annually? I don't know the aggregate, but we're moving about 144 million gallons are being pumped daily from the foreign water supplies. So that's probably a good surrogate.

These are for the Oahu system. We can get you that data.

Mr. TAM. But it could take Oahu, the most popular island where you have a more centralized system that's probably a good number.

There's about a hundred million gallons going out into the water into the ocean. As Gary Hill indicated yesterday, waste water is simply water or it could be waste. There's things we put into it, we can simply take those things out.

There's methane. There's phosphates. There's a lot of things to be taken out. Those are separate income streams that, properly organized, could then become actually a way to reduce your overall costs.

So the point of it is conservation is, as been indicated, is the single most cost effective way to deal with water energy. There have been studies by—at this University over the last 15 or 20 years. This is not new information. Looking at the cost benefit of investing in watershed manifers as a way of increasing supply while the technical aspects of that would require looking at their papers, essentially if you have a choice between building a new well which is going to move motors when down further and requires more and more pipelines or managing the watershed which then can capture more of that rainfall, put it back into the ground. That's the real supply side economics.

That's where you're actually increasing, for example an aquifer from say, 10 million gallons to 12 million. You still use your existing infrastructure to take on one, as opposed to building a well and take out one more of a $10 mine. So the watershed management has multiple benefits aside from what just happens on the surface.

Aside from the fact they're hiring young people to go out and work in the natural resources. You're actually increasing your supply. As the indications are often to climate—the university and elsewhere the rainfall pattern around the Hawaiian Islands are indicating that the clouds that fit the windward side of the mountains where you have to—our water are getting thinner both pressure down and pressure up from the heat. Therefore the amount of water hitting the mountains which is the source of our rainfall that caused a thinner—that cost more and more money.

USGS indicates that in the last 80 years primarily from the 1940s to the present that aggregate stream flows now 20 to 22 percent aggregate rainfall just in the last 30 years it's down 10 to 12 percent. If those patterns continue we're going to have less water in the streams, less water in the ground. To take advantage of what we can do in the forests, bring back native plants, cut down the invasive because as this happens, by the way, the invasives move up. Invasives are now taking over our forests.

That trend is very dangerous because they have high, rapid transpiration rates. They do not put the water back in the ground. The Strawberry Guava throughout the islands, that is going to—that is really more and more mountain. If you talk to Senator Ruderman and—observed in his lifetime different kinds of weeds and invasives that he saw—topography. That's happening everywhere.

So those phenomenon while not by themselves spectacular, in the aggregate have a major impact on our water supply.

We would encourage you to look at conservation measures just as a cost efficient method to do this.

The last thing I would like to say is that water integrates Ag, waste water use, water for consumption and the energy costs so that it integrates this in ways that others things do not. So saving water distribution is a way of paying down other costs and allowing greater efficiencies.

The last point I guess I would make would be that we've dealt with this on a regional basis. If we do, simply do this on a bilateral contract basis we will not have the efficiencies. So we're going to do waste water management, central water, for example, there would be savings in different places. But we need to figure out a way to allocate those savings and allocate those budgets in a way so everybody gets to play.

I would encourage you to look at the work that the Army is doing at Schofield Air—and should be a model for the rest of this——

Thank you for your time.

[The prepared statement of Mr. Tam follows:]

PREPARED STATEMENT OF WILLIAM M. TAM, DEPUTY DIRECTOR, HAWAII COMMISSION ON WATER RESOURCE MANAGEMENT, DEPARTMENT OF LAND AND NATURAL RESOURCES (DLNR), HONOLULU, HI

Aloha,

On behalf of the Hawaii Department of Land and Natural Resources and the State Commission on Water Resource Management, thank you for inviting us to speak with you about Successes and Challenges in Meeting Sustainability Goals for Water in Hawaii.[1]

My name is William Tam. I am Deputy Director, Commission on Water Resource Management ("Commission"), Hawaii Department of Land and Natural Resources.

I. INTRODUCTION

The Hawaii State Constitution (article XI, §7) (1978) and the State Water Code (Haw. Rev. Stat. chap 174C) (1987) charge the State with a dual mandate: provide for reasonable and beneficial uses of water and protect public trust water resources for this and for future generations. Integrating reasonable and beneficial uses and long term resource protection requires sustainable water supplies.

The challenge of climate change to Hawaii's water resources will alter how we manage our natural resources-and ourselves—for decades to come. This is an epochal change and a fundamental shift to a new paradigm. The hard path of big supply projects will no longer meet our needs. Not only will the infrastructure change. The way we use water will change. In some areas, we are approaching "peak water." So different water qualities will be needed to satisfy different kinds of demand. And it will be more decentralized and distributed because the cost of energy will require it. It is time for a twenty-first century water policy?[2]

II. CLIMATE CHANGE

The World Economic Forum Global Risks 2014 identified "water crises" and "failure of climate change mitigation and adaptation" as third and fifth, respectively, in its rank ordering of the ten global risks of highest concern in 2014.[3] They considered the risks to have a high likelihood and to have a high impact. The report concluded that (1) trust is necessary if stakeholders are to work together; (2) long-term thinking is a prerequisite to any approach to global risks; (3) collaborative multi-stakeholder action is required as no single entity has the tools and the authority to tackle systematic risks; and (4) new governance models are needed.

In Hawaii, all water is local. Hawaii faces climate change-related impacts on our water resources different in kind from our sister states on the continental United States. Even dry states may (under certain circumstances) transport fresh water across state borders. Hawaii does not have that option. Each island is on its own when it comes to water. There is no Plan B to import or transport fresh water in life sustaining quantities. Each island must adapt to the uncertainties of climate change in its own way.

---

[1] The Hawaii Commission on Water Resources Management website http://dlnr.hawaii.gov/cwrm/ provides extensive information about the Commission's work and links to many primary and secondary sources.

[2] Juliet Christian-Smith and Peter Gleick, A Twenty-First Century U.S. Water Policy, Oxford University Press (2012)

[3] World Economic Forum Global Risks 2014 (www.weforum.org/risks)

The observed trends in climate change and projections of reduced future freshwater supplies make it imperative that Hawaii 1) aggressively pursue water conservation; 2) explore and expand the use of reused and reclaimed water; and 3) prepare for both persistent drought conditions (on the leeward sides of the islands) and less frequent, but larger rain events that run off quickly, fail to recharge the aquifers, transport soil onto near shore reefs; and 4) collect reliable hydrologic data to understand and monitor conditions in order to respond nimbly to new conditions.

In the future, the leeward sides of all the major Hawaiian Islands are likely to be even drier. It is critical to collect and expand our collection of hydrologic data to refine future projections.

III. SECURE WATER AMENDMENTS ACT OF 2014 (S.2019): CONSERVING WATER RESPOURCES; PROMOTING SUSTAINABILITY

First, Senator, we would like to thank you for introducing the Secure Water Amendments Act of 2014 (S.2019). This Bill will allow Hawaii to compete for grants under the Department of Interior's WaterSMART Program, increase funding for drought projects, provide resources for better data collection and analysis of water supply. This will help Hawaii improve our water supplies' resiliency and sustainability. Hawai'i will become eligible for WaterSMART cost share Water and Energy Efficiency Grants, System Optimization Review Grants, Advanced Water Treatment and Pilot and Demonstration Project Grants, and Grants to Develop Climate Analysis Tools. Water resource stakeholders will be able to partner and collaborate with the Department of Interior.

The four County departments of water supply, the County wastewater departments, the Commission on Water Resource Management, the Department of Land and Natural Resources, the University of Hawaii, the Department of Agriculture, the Department of Hawaiian Home Lands, and other water-related entities will benefit from this legislation.

IV. WASTEWATER REUSE AND STORMWATER RECLAMATION

Wastewater reuse and stormwater reclamation are growing rapidly (especially in the West) as communities realize that every part of the water cycle is valuable, just mislabeled.[4] But large- scale wastewater reuse and stormwater reclamation are relatively new in Hawaii and not widely understood. As Hawaii's population and water demands grow and water supplies come under new pressures, wastewater reuse and stormwater capture will be key components in sustainable water resource management for non-potable needs.

OPPORTUNITY AND CHALLENGE

In 2008, the Hawaii Commission on Resources Management in partnership with the U.S. Bureau of Reclamation completed an appraisal-level study of opportunities statewide for the large-scale stormwater reclamation. Of twenty opportunities identified statewide, stormwater reclamation and reuse at Wheeler Army Air Base and Schofield Barracks (Wheeler) was determined to have the most stakeholder support and greatest likelihood for success. A pilot project at Wheeler could potentially use a significant amount of existing infrastructure for collection, treatment, storage, and conveyance of stormwater. The idea is to collect stormwater from the approximately 190 acres of runway and impervious surfaces at Wheeler airfield, where average annual rainfall is 40 to 50 inches/ year. The Schofield Barracks Wastewater Treatment Facility (located at Wheeler) contains several unused clarifiers that could be used to treat and improve the stormwater quality. An unused pipeline extends from the Wheeler property to nine 1.8 million gallon (16.2 million gallon total) underground former oil storage reservoirs at Waikakalaua Fuel Annex. Waiahole Ditch, or a parallel pipeline in the ditch easement, could convey the stormwater to downstream irrigation users, which include agricultural lands, golf courses, and other green spaces. An extension of the pipeline would allow surplus stormwater to be used to recharge the Pearl Harbor Aquifer or, further makai, the Ewa Caprock Aquifer.

Commission records indicate that over 25 million gallons per day of high-quality potable groundwater from the Wahiawa and Waipahu-Waiawa Aquifer System Areas are currently permitted for non-potable uses. If these non-potable uses could be converted to non-potable sources, high-quality groundwater could be conserved for potable uses. In addition, development of this opportunity will help to meet Clean Water Act requirements. Currently, stormwater from Wheeler enters Waikele Stream, eventually discharging to the West Loch of Pearl Harbor. Both of these

---

[4] "Water Reuse: Potential for Expanding the Nation's Water Supply through Reuse of Municipal Wastewater," National Research Council, National Academy of Science (2012) (http://www.nap.edu)

water bodies are identified as impaired on the Department of Health §303(d) list. Implementation of Total Maximum Daily Loads (TMDLs) to receiving waters by the Department of Health will eventually require a higher level of treatment for stormwater.[5] The treatment required to comply with TMDLs will potentially offset the treatment required for other uses, particularly irrigation.

The State is currently investigating how non-potable water could be developed regionally in Central Oahu. Land use is in transition. With the decline of plantation agriculture, vast tracts of former sugarcane lands lie fallow. There are plans for increased agricultural activity in the Kunia Road corridor, expansion of military housing at U.S. Army Schofield Barracks, and proposals for new urban developments. There is significant non-potable water demand associated with each of these planned activities.

There are also a number of sources of non-potable water in the Central Oahu. In addition to stormwater, 1) there are two wastewater treatment plants, Schofield and Wahiawa that are capable of producing R-1 water; 2) Lake Wilson, which has a current capacity of 2.5 billion gallons and a pass through stream flow estimated at 36 million gallons per day; 3) the Waiahole Ditch; 4) new wastewater treatment facilities associated with new developments; and 5) new re- sourcing treatment facilities that could divert and treat wastewater from existing pipelines near or on-site for landscaping or agricultural use (thereby saving energy costs of pumping water miles away to large treatment plants).

V. COORDINATE AND INTEGRATE WATER RESOURCE PLANNING ACROSS JURISDICTIONS ON A LIFE-CYCLE, TRIPLE BOTTOM LINE BASIS

There is a need for new, coordinated, and integrated water resource planning across jurisdictions, and on a life-cycle, triple bottom line basis.[6]. If water supply planning and implementation continue in a piecemeal fashion, the opportunity to partner and leverage resources may be lost. This may result in higher capital and operating costs, lost efficiencies, and unfavorable outcomes. By taking a regional approach and involving multiple stakeholders, there may be new economies in savings and avoided costs. Specifically, benefits and costs may be redistributed geographically or across time to enable an integrated plan to succeed where none of the component parts alone would start, let alone survive.

For example, reusing wastewater in Central Oahu could reduce the size and capital costs to expand the planned secondary treatment facility at the Honouliuli Wastewater Treatment Plant. That could also reduce operations and energy costs to pump the wastewater to Honouliuli.

Through a regional plan, there may be a combined benefit among entities that would not pencil out financially for any single party acting independently.

Given the many interested stakeholders in the area, there is a need to engage all stakeholders—landowners, farmers, developers, the military, wastewater treatment plant operators, Board of Water Supply, Department of Health, and others in a collaborative planning effort that looks at all resources, all potential demand, and identifies solutions in the best interests of the community and the State. The Commission wants to ensure that water supply, wastewater, and stormwater planning in Central Oahu proceed in a way that can address these issues and concerns early in the process and to mitigate any foreseeable conflicts. The Commission is working to finish its non-potable water planning in the fall, 2014.

Pending completion of this work, developing and implementing a proof of concept pilot project is important to demonstrate the feasibility of stormwater reclamation and reuse and establish its viability, associated technical issues, costs and budget, and build support for the larger effort. This regional undertaking will require close working relationships among federal, state, county, and private parties. Above all, it will require leadership and innovation.

VI. FULL CYCLE ENERGY COSTS OF WATER

The cost to pump groundwater, transport it to end users, move it again as sewage (by gravity piping and force mains) to wastewater treatment plants, remove the chemicals and solids, force it into long ocean outfalls, and comply with the Clean

---

[5] In September, 2012, EPA released is updated 2012 Guidelines for Water Reuse, U.S. EPA, EPA/600/R-12/6/18 (2012)

[6] "Triple Bottom Line" refers to an accounting framework for sustainability that includes financial, social, and environmental measures (often referred to as People, Planet, and Profits). While the metrics for each may differ, projects may nonetheless be compared on each alone. This creates a mechanism to evaluate the ramifications of alternative decisions from a truly long term perspective much as a series of cash flows may be compared by reducing each to its present value.

Water Act is expensive. While the energy costs of water are appreciated on the mainland,[7] they have received little attention in Hawaii.

In the first 11 months of FY 2012, the Honolulu Board of Water Supply paid approximately $26.8 million for 87.9 million kilowatt hours to pump 143 million gallons I day for one year. That is about $187,500 to pump one (1) mgd for one year.

In FY 2013, the City and County of Honolulu Department of Environmental Services paid approximately $24.3 million for about 74 million kilowatt hours to treat and pump about 99.4 mgd of sewage for a year. That is about $244,000 I year per one (1) mgd of sewage treated.

Combined, the BWS and Environmental Services' energy cost to pump, transport, treat, and dispose of one mgd of water is about $431,500 /year. And that is just the electrical costs. It does not include the capital, the infrastructure, the human labor, or the environmental costs. Imagine securing the service that potable water provides in a whole new way. Calculate the opportunity costs of leaving potable (and future drinking) water in the ground (the best reservoir there is- as Arizona's groundwater recharge project demonstrates) and not pumping (lower energy costs). But the overall plan may only succeed if this savings can be allocated and distributed to other regional parties on an overall cost efficient basis. There will simply not be enough bi-lateral contracts to make the whole work. It requires a regional approach.

It goes without saying that the Uniform Plumbing Code ("UPC") and International Green Construction Code ("IGCC"), as well as local county ordinances provide important institutional pathways to the day to day implementation of real conservation. It is through these retrofitting mechanisms that old (as well as new) infrastructure is realigned in more efficient directions. Ironically, the cost I benefit payback period for investing in many of these retrofits is often less than one year and it generates new work for skilled labor in small and medium sized operations. One perverse effect of rising energy costs is it makes investment and rapid changes in new efficiencies more economic.

VII. DROUGHT PLANNING, MITIGATION, AND RESPONSE

The Commission is the lead agency for drought planning in Hawaii. The Hawaii Drought Council helps to coordinate drought mitigation and response activities across the state. In 2005, the Commission developed the Hawaii Drought Plan which led to working with drought stakeholders in each county to develop four County Drought Mitigation Strategies. The County Drought Mitigation Strategies identify projects to improve drought preparedness and resilience in the water supply; agriculture & commerce; and environment, public health and safety sectors.

The Hawaii Water Resources Act of 2000 (P.L. 106-566, as amended) made Hawaii eligible for U.S. Department of Interior, Bureau of Reclamation programs for drought relief and drought planning. Hawaii was able to benefit from these programs during the droughts in the last decade through emergency drought assistance and planning assistance from the Bureau of Reclamation. The authority for emergency drought relief (Title I of P.L. 102-250, as amended) expired on September 30, 2012. Reauthorization of this authority and appropriation of program funding could help stakeholders in Hawaii to better cope with drought.

There are several federal agencies that offer programmatic assistance for drought mitigation and response, including U.S. Department of Interior's Bureau of Reclamation and U.S. Department of Agriculture's Natural Resources Conservation Service, Farm Service Agency, Rural Development Program and Risk Management Agency. The respective County Drought Mitigation Strategies have drought mitigation projects in need of funding sources and could qualify for one or more of the programs offered by these agencies, should funding opportunities become available.

Hawaii also benefits from the work of the National Oceanic and Atmospheric Administration's National Integrated Drought Information System (NIDIS). Continued support for NIDIS is important for maintaining a drought early warning system and for delivering products, tools, resources and programs to assist drought stakeholders to prepare for and mitigate the impacts of drought across the country.

VIII. NEED FOR INCREASED CLIMATE AND HYDROLOGIC MONITORING AND RESEARCH

Hawaii's climate is extremely diverse. Micro-climates are the rule rather than the exception. We have rainforests and deserts, alpine mountains and coastal plains. Annual precipitation can vary by more than 100 inches/year in a span of just a few

---

[7] "Implications of Future Water Supply Sources for Energy Demands," Heather Cooley (Pacific Institute) and Robert Wilkinson (UC Santa Barbara), WateReuse Research Foundation and Bureau of Reclamation (DOl) (2012); "Energy Down the Drain- The Hidden Costs of California's Water Supply," NRDC and Pacific Institute (August 2004)

miles. Rain gages and stream gages allow us to monitor trends in these elements over time. In order to get a clear picture of climate change, there needs to be monitoring with long periods of record and sufficient geographical coverage to represent our different climate regions across the state. The number of stream gages in Hawaii has declined from over 197 (1966) to only 59 in 2012. Rainfall stations have decreased from a peak of over 1000 in 1968 to around 340 in 2007. This decline in monitoring is leaving gaps in the data at a time when we need this long-term data the most.

Stream gages operated by the U.S. Geological Survey are funded on a cost-share basis with cooperators, who are mainly state and county agencies. The recent fiscal crisis caused these cooperators to reduce funding for data collection resulting in the loss of important stream gaging stations. The National Weather Service administers a cooperative observer program in Hawaii, which comprises its volunteer rain gage network. Hawaii's sugar plantations were prolific rainfall observers. Since the plantations closed, the network of rainfall stations declined precipitously. It is important to re-establish both stream gages and rainfall stations in key climatic regions where there is a long period of record of observations. The continuation of hydrologic data collection and analysis is fundamental in monitoring how Hawaii's climate is changing and to ascertain the impacts of climate change on our water availability both now and in the future.

Section 9506, Secure Water Act of 2009 establishes a Climate Change and Water Intergovernmental Panel in order to address the issue of data gaps in current water monitoring networks and how to improve data collection to better monitor and analyze water resources.

Section 9507 of the Act authorizes the implementation of programs to enhance water data collection by the U.S. Geological Survey.

Congress needs to appropriate sufficient funds to implement the provisions described above and for the U.S. Geological Survey in Hawaii to increase the number of stream gages in Hawaii, especially where critical, long-term stream gages have been discontinued.

Congress also needs to appropriate fund to increase the number of Hawaiian rainfall stations and reestablish important rainfall stations with long periods of record through the Pacific Islands Climate Science Center or the University of Hawaii.

Ensuring that hydrologic data collection continues in Hawaii is the only way to effectively monitor and analyze the impacts of climate change on our precious fresh water resources. This essential data set will benefit many sectors of the community—researchers and resource managers alike, including the University of Hawaii, U.S. Geological Survey, Hawaii Department of Land and Natural Resources, and many others.

IX. ACTIVE LEADERSIDP AND ENGAGEMENT ACROSS JURISDICTIONS

The key is active leadership. Money and legislation may be slow and hard to secure. But getting people from all levels of government, across multiple functions, and in conjunction with private actors to sit down and talk with one another requires only active leadership and personal time. It is the human contact that opens the doors. We have the means to communicate with one another. It is not expensive. It just requires convening meetings or hearings (like this one) to highlight innovations, encourage collaboration, re-imagine smaller more dynamic on-site systems, and share opportunities.

Agency Collaboration

Protect water resources through accelerated collaborative effort by City, State and Federal agencies.

Planning

Analyze true life cycle costs/value of water resources across jurisdictions, the full hydrologic cycle, and functions so that efficiencies and costs can be realized across multiple users. Compare alternative scenarios, including the cost of current course. Integrate energy costs into all water analysis. Integrate analysis and synchronize plans across all levels of government. Examine regulatory changes (practices and rules) needed to realize the proposals outlined here.

Watershed protection

Expand forest and agricultural public/private partnerships to combat invasive species, capture and enhance groundwater resources, restore native plants, and increase resilience to climate change.[8] Prevent runoff and pollution in ahupua'a and watershed area across jurisdictions (using mauka to makai approach)

Infrastructure improvements and controls

Investigate and support treating wastewater to R-1 for reuse from state, county, federal, and private facilities. Capture and reclaim storm water, grey water, and rainwater to replace potable water use in urban and agricultural applications. Expand grading and agricultural soil conservation efforts. Increase efficiencies in agricultural irrigation practices. Decentralize and relocate new and renovated infrastructure away from coastlines

Finance

Explore ways to engage private funding sources.[9] Insurance companies calculate risk and have good reason to search out risk reduction strategies. Develop new pricing structures. Publish combined water & energy triple bottom line accounting for all projects.

Multi-Agency Coordination Group

Establish multi-agency coordination group with a specific mandate to analyze how to carry out the tasks described here (including how to engage private funding sources). Set a deadline to report back to this Committee in one year (May, 2015).

Mid-Course Corrections: Flexible, Adaptive, and Responsive

Increasingly, water, energy, and natural resource problems combine in new and faster ways. Old, isolated approaches fail to capture the interaction or the complexity of problems, their solutions, or their urgency. We need more mid-course corrections. Institutions designed 20-40 years ago need to work horizontally across jurisdictions and in near real time. Specifically, federal agencies (especially EPA and COE, but also USFWS and NOAA) need to get closer to the management problems and help States be flexible and more adaptive. Navigating requires regular mid-course corrections and quick feedback loops.

X. GOING FORWARD

Climate change poses great uncertainties and risks to sustainable water supplies. Water conservation, development of non-potable alternatives, integrated actions across multiple jurisdictions, drought planning, and mixed public-private financing and watershed protection require direct active leadership and attention.

Hawaii is developing a number of initiatives that are still in their early stages. We would appreciate the opportunity to provide the Subcommittee with a more detailed account of these activities. To that end, we request that the record in this matter be kept open until April30, 2014 to supplement the testimony provided here.

Thank you for the opportunity to share our views. We look forward to working with this Subcommittee and our federal partners to achieve a sustainable water future for Hawaii.

Senator SCHATZ. Thank you very much.

Dr. Pauley.

STATEMENT OF STEPHEN M. PAULEY, MD, PRESIDENT, EDWIN W. PAULEY FOUNDATION, KETCHUM, ID

Mr. PAULEY. Thank you, Senator Schatz, for this opportunity to recommend that Coconut Island, Kane'ohe Bay, Oahu, Hawaii serve as a living example for sustainable systems that will stimulate the building and implementation of similar systems by others in the Hawaiian Islands, most of North America and the Pacific Rim.

When Coconut Island was gifted to the University of Hawaii Foundation the Pauley intended that in addition to the green sciences already in place at HIMB, the Hawaii Institute of Marine

[8] "Natural Infrastructure- Investing in Forested Landscapes for Source Water Protection;" World Resources Institute (2012).

[9] "Financing Green Urban Infrastructure" (OECD Regional Development Working Papers 2012/10; http://dc.doi .org/10.17875k92p0c6j6ro-en); Creating Clean Water Cash Flows- Developing Private Markets of Green Stormwater Infrastructure in Philadelphia (NRDC January 2013; http://www.nrdc.org/water/stormwater/files/green-infrastructure-pa-report.pdf)

Biology, that the island would become a model for sustainability. In my dedication speech in 1998, when I dedicated the island along with a newly built marine lab I said the following.

"If we can relate the first rate science being done at this new lab to improving ecosystems in this bay, the Hawaiian Islands and the Pacific Ocean, if we can make Coconut Island a model for sustainable living, if we can leave the comfort zone to our narrow disciplines to relate our science to others in the community, and to the diverse fields of humanities, of the humanities, if we can find the courage to shape public policy to improve our environment and if by doing these things we end up with a healthier ecosphere, through your efforts to reconnect people to the natural world, than our gifts to you in Hawaii will have real meaning, not only to our granddaughters, Hannah and Brooke." We have 2 more since then. "But to our future set of generation."

That was in 1998. Hannah is now 17, 18 and ready to go to college. The point being, it's been a long time.

[Laughter.]

Mr. PAULEY. Coconut Island long range development in 1998 was drafted by 16 leaders from the University of Hawaii and surrounding communities, approved by the UH Board of Regents, cochaired by then UH President Ken Mortimer and me.

The mission statement reads, "To promote the stewardship of the living oceans, restore, preserve and sustain marine ecosystems in Hawaii and the Pacific Rim to integrate scientific research, community involvement, education and example at Coconut Island."

Almost 16 years have passed and those goals have been minimally achieved. This has been a disappointment to the Board of Directors of the Pauley Foundation and the Pauley family. To many at UH who also see the potential for the island to serve as an example for sustainable systems that include the use of solar and wind energy, fresh water catchment, natural sewage treatment and the use of sustainable building materials.

While first rate marine science is routinely conducted at HIMB the island's overall potential is still lacking. The reasons for the lack of concerted action are many, most are budget related. There has been a lack of continuity at UH. Four presidents have served UH over the past 16 years. There needs to be both a political and strategic will to adhere to the zoning of environmental sustainability emissions stated in the 1998 Coconut Island long range development plan.

Senator Schatz, you have firsthand knowledge of Coconut Island's potential. We both served on the Board of Directors for the Center for a Sustainable Future. The organization was founded by former dean of SOEST, Dr. Barry Raleigh.

CSF was funded by private foundations and donors. We studied issues such as coastal pollution, coral beaching, reduced fish populations, aqua cultures and strategies for the use of biofuels to replace dependency on imported oil. We also studied other environmental problems in Hawaii and the Pacific Rim. But funding fell short when it came to implementing sustainable systems. CFS was disbanded when Dr. Raleigh retired as Dean of SOEST.

So the specific request that I am making of the committee since we've been unable to achieve the progress on any other basis is to implement the Coconut Island master plan of 1998.

No. 1, build sustainable energy, water and building system on the island so that the island can serve as an example of what to do correctly in the era of climate change, dependency on fossil fuels warming oceans and loss of coral reefs and fisheries.

No. 2, build a conference center and visitor housing. This is all in the master plan. To bring together others in Hawaii and the Pacific Rim to study environmental issues such as food shortages, depleted fisheries, climate change and shoreline flooding. These are all issues obviously we all know about that threaten coastal communities.

I thank you for this opportunity to state my views.

[The prepared statement of Mr. Pauley follows:]

PREPARED STATEMENT OF STEPHEN M. PAULEY, MD, PRESIDENT, EDWIN W. PAULEY FOUNDATION, KETCHUM, ID

Thank you Senator Schatz for this opportunity to recommend that Coconut Island, Kaneohe, Oahu, Hawaii, serve as a living example for sustainable systems that would stimulate the building and implementation of similar systems by others in the Hawaiian Islands, coastal North America, and the Pacific Rim.

When Coconut Island was gifted to the University of Hawaii Foundation, the Pauley Foundation intended that in addition to the marine sciences already in place at the Hawaii Institute of Marine Biology (HIMB), that the island would become a model for sustainability.

In my dedication speech in 1998, when I dedicated the island along with a newly built marine lab I said the following:

"If we can relate the first rate science being done at this new lab to improving ecosystems in this bay, the Hawaiian Islands & the Pacific Ocean; if we can make Coconut Island a model for sustainable living; if we can leave the comfort zones of our narrow disciplines to relate our science to others in the community and to the diverse fields of the humanities; if we can find the courage to shape public policy to improve our environment, and if by doing these things we end up with a healthier ecosphere through your efforts to re-connect people to the natural world, then our gifts to you and Hawaii will have real meaning not only to grand daughters Hannah and Brooke, but to our future 7th generation."

The Coconut Island Long Range Development Plan of 1998 was drafted by 16 leaders from the University of Hawaii and surrounding communities, approved by the UH Board of Regents, and co chaired by then UH President Ken Mortimer and me. The Mission Statement reads:

"To promote the stewardship of the living oceans, restore, preserve, and sustain marine ecosystems in Hawaii and the Pacific Rim through integrated scientific research, community involvement, education, and example at Coconut Island." (1998 Coconut Island Long Range Development Plan)

Almost 16 years have passed and those goals have been minimally achieved. This has been a disappointment to the board of directors of the Pauley Foundation, to the Pauley family, and to many at UH who also see the potential for the island to serve as an example for sustainable systems that include the use of solar and wind energy, fresh water catchment, natural sewage treatment, and the use of sustainable building materials.

While first rate marine science is routinely conducted at HIMB, the island's overall potential is still lacking. The reasons for lack of concerted action are many. Most are budget related. There has been a lack of continuity at UH; four presidents have served UH over the past 16 yrs. There needs to be both a political and strategic will to adhere to the zoning and environmental sustainability missions stated in the 1998 Coconut Island Long Range Development Plan.

Senator Schatz, you have firsthand knowledge of Coconut Island's potential. We both served on the board of directors for the Center for a Sustainable Future (CSF). The organization was founded by former Dean of the School of Ocean Engineering

Science and Technology (SOEST) at UH, Dr Barry Raliegh. CSF was funded by private foundations and donors. We studied issues such as coastal pollution, coral bleaching, reduced fish populations, aquaculture, strategies for the use of biofuels to replace dependency on imported oil, and other environmental problems in Hawaii and the Pacific Rim. But funding fell short when it came to implementing sustainable systems. CSF disbanded when Dr Raleigh retired as Dean of SOEST at the University.

Specific Request of this committee

Congressional funding for Coconut Island is requested to implement the Coconut Island Master Plan of 1998:

1) build sustainable energy, water, and building systems on Coconut Island, Kaneohe, Oahu so that the island can serve as an example of what to do correctly in the era of climate change, dependency on fossil fuels, warming oceans, and loss of coral reefs and fisheries;

2) build a conference center and visitor housing to bring together others in Hawaii and the Pacific Rim to study environmental issues such as climate change, food shortages, depleted fisheries, and coastal flooding— all issues that threaten coastal communities;

Senator SCHATZ. Thank all of the testifiers. I do have a number of questions.

I'll start with Mr. Tam and, I think, Ms. Meguro. This is a general question because you know that I understand the water and power nexus. What I am still needing help with is that because we have the old, physical infrastructure and old statutory, regulatory infrastructure and old ways of doing things, that, you know, I had a workshop 6 or 8 months ago where we talked about this.

I have very capable staff. I have access to all kinds of experts. Yet, the question of how, exactly, to manifest the thinking that's expressed at this panel in terms of making sure that we make holistic decisions. There seems to still be a gap in terms of what changes, either at the regulatory or policymaking level, need to be made.

I understand that projects can be done more intelligently. I understand that at the building level that people ought to be smarter about things.

But given that, you have boards and departments of water supply and then you have electric utility companies and sort of, never the twain shall meet, except with the concept which is that utilities use a lot of water and electric utilities use a lot of water and then, of course, the water utilities use a lot of electricity. So it's all intuitive except that in terms of effectuating long term, holistic planning, it's not at all clear to me what kinds of changes at the policy level need to be made.

Mr. TAM. Thank you, Senator.

The first act is going to be an act of imagination because we have to understand how the water moves. Once you understand how the water moves, you've got to ask the question how might it move differently.

I'll give you a simple example. If the Coal Rich project proceeds they will have to build, under current plans, a pipeline from the new facilities or new subdivision down to the transfer station and then over Honolulu-Uley. That pipeline alone is $40 million.

If instead they were to be asked or if they chose to build an R1 facility so remembering our bio-rec facility, they could treat the water there to an R1 quality, use it on their lands, use it on adjacent lands, provide irrigation water that's non potable, for example, to the Patsy Mink Park which is right below that. Currently the border up supply pumps about a million gallons a day to irrigate potable water to irrigate land.

If that could be done with R1 water you can save the potable water by pumping a million gallons a day. You could save——

Senator SCHATZ. Would the county or State laws need to be changed in order for them to be able to do this?

Mr. TAM. I don't think so. I think this is more an action of and I don't have a direct answer, maybe some type of biospecs, but I think it's more a decisionmaking across the groups. People might have to sit down and talk about it.

Senator SCHATZ. But this would be the Land Use Commission requiring or the Department of Planning and Permitting do these?

Mr. TAM. I don't think so. I think—and I defer to the sum of the county process. But I think it's more a matter of just figuring out the pathway forward and maybe some permitting requirements. It depends on each project.

But I think in the first instance it's sitting down and getting a plan figured out among people who will be affected. But I just wanted to take this as an example. If you leave a million gallons in the ground which is your best reservoir, you don't have to pump it.

Those savings are important. Now those savings will be realized primarily by the Board of Water Supply. The question is if you have a regional plan is can you reallocate those savings to some other part of the property so then you make cost efficiency work.

Now the Board of Water Supply, of course, will tell you they've got to have all that savings. But if they're going to play with everybody else it's important that they shared some fraction to make other, less efficient parts of the plan work.

Senator SCHATZ. Right. But it's not trivial to—and I understand you're giving me a specific example, but it's, sort of, not trivial at all that we're sitting here not clear whether we need changes in the law or not and not clear at all whether or not this is a question of leadership or a question of policy. I presume it's both.

But it seems to me that we are, sort of, knocking around on this issue because it's so obviously the smart thing to do. Yet, the mechanics are not, you know, well articulated quite yet.

Mr. TAM. I would make a suggestion and it's in my written testimony on this point, actually, that there be a coordinating committee organized between the mayor or the Governor with the relevant people involved and come back and report to this committee at the end of the year so we have a forcing mechanism and come back with those specific suggestions that would make a difference in those areas.

I think that's—then we could get down to what the legal changes might have to be, what the purveying schemes are, but they vary by topography.

For example, right now the Army Corps or rather the Army drew a contract and is working with aqua engineers to take all their own water. They use it for landscaping. People are going to move some R1 water to Kaneohe to some of the farmers down there. That would be a different kind of arrangement with the county.

So there are specific permitting requirements. But I don't think we can give you that answer right now.

Ms. MEGURO. So I've been trying to chase down the same question in the last maybe, 6 months. I would say that answer is a little fuzzy. But I can tell you what I've learned so far.

First, I think there is a body who has been looking into this, the U.S. Green Building Council, Hawaii Chapter, Advocacy Committee. They have been reviewing some of the plumbing codes for recommendation for adoption by the State and counties.

So as I understand they are looking at both the international green construction code and the uniform plumbing code 2012 as potential overlays or for full adoption by the counties. I don't think that has come to a conclusion yet, in my understanding.

Next, I was wondering if there was any hang up in the Department of Health, if for some reason their water quality standards that might be holding us back.

My read of the codes so far, it looks like the Department of Health is willing to review design projects on a case by case basis and that that was not the hurdle. It sounds inefficient to, kind of, go on for every or review every design project on a case by case basis. But it was not the road block.

One of the things that I did hear that is not necessarily a road block, but is definitely, slows us down, is a Hawaii Administrative Rule which requires building projects to hook up, pay to hook up to the sewer if it is available at your site. If you have a water treatment plant offsite or a system onsite that is sufficient for your building or set of buildings, then is it really necessary to pay to hook up to the sewer?

So that's, I think, one challenge that design teams are facing.

Thanks.

Senator SCHATZ. Thank you very much.

Chairman Morita.

Ms. MORITA. I just wanted to point out that I think a lot of the solutions to this is dealing with cultural changes within departments. Every department is so siloed. We need to pick up the phone and call each other and find out what's happening. We have been.

Using the public benefit fee we've been delving into the energy water nexus. Again, using the public benefit fee we have a publication coming out on water, waste water best practices, that will be distributed to the boards of water, even though we don't regulate them, as well as the private water sewer companies that we are—that we do regulate. So there's some cross pollination, pollinization going on between departments.

Thanks to DLNR providing us with information, also Department of Health, we at least have staff talking to each other about how do we gain these additional efficiencies and how do we take these direct and indirect savings from designing within a system approach?

Senator SCHATZ. Thank you.

In the interest of time I'd like to move on.

Mr. Rue, I appreciate your testimony. I appreciate that you delineated some ways that we can be helpful in terms of making sure that the Federal Government programs that already exist are coordinating best with the city and county of Honolulu on your projects.

Which programs do you rely upon the most in terms of Federal revenue streams or individuals who are collaborating with you?

Mr. RUE. Sure.

I should confess that before joining, rejoining the city a few months ago, I did work as a consultant for several of the Federal agencies and help work on those programs myself. So I understand the inner mechanics a little bit.

We do—we use a lot of funding from DOT, you know, in addition to the huge amounts that we are getting for the transit system itself, we get money for bus systems, for road repairs and building. Have a good working relationship there.

We are in touch with the more innovative folks in the Livability program, both here locally as well as, you know, in DC and certainly get some wisdom from them. We are competing for a Tiger grant, you know, that's due out now, in the next month. So, it will be, you know, certainly pursuing competitive grants as well.

With EPA we have had a strong relationship with their smart growth program, you know, since actually before it was. We had an EPA site visit in 2004 that was even before the Environmental Department was really kicked off. They've done several workshops, many of them through the sea grant program. I've been involved in a lot of them over the years, even when I was in Ohio.

So there's a strong relationship there, particularly with sea grant on a lot of community designed issues.

We recently applied for a Brown Fuels funding grant and we have a good relationship with those folks as well.

Then with HUD we did receive a little over 2 million for the HUD Community Challenge grant. We set up an equitable housing fund. So we have a really good relationship with HUD, Office of Sustainable Housing and Communities, as well as with the ongoing regular statutory funding. I think one of their deputies was here recently working with our team on the homelessness issues and, you know, that kind of statutory funding

Senator SCHATZ. Thank you very much.

This goes for all the panelists and anybody in this room who is working in this phase. I know most of you already know this, but certainly our staff and our office and committee stands ready to assist you in all of the programs and projects that you're working on.

Dr. Pauley, I want to talk to you about the master plan for Coconut Island. I appreciate your dawet pursuit of this vision and your relentlessness because I know that it's been, especially recently, quite challenging.

My question for you, specifically is does the 1998 master plan, sort of, hold up? Does it need to be revised in order to attract the kind of leadership and funding that is required or is it essentially ready to go and just requiring some political will and some resources?

Mr. PAULEY. I think it's ready to go. There's really, all the components are there based on the things we've been hearing the last few days, water, sewer, thinking of the natural sewer system, solar panels. You know, we've been talking about solar for a long time out there. It just hasn't happened for one reason or another.

So I think it's ready to go.

Senator SCHATZ. Are we in arrears with respect to infrastructure, I mean, basic infrastructure at this point? Is there some? Do you have some sense of what the price tag would be?

Mr. PAULEY. At one time we thought that would be about $13 million. The sea walls are all falling down and I know that Governor Abercrombie and Clayton, he found some money in the State this year to build some of that up to help the infrastructure. We certainly appreciate that.

When I say we are really not—anybody to call the shots anymore since you gave the gift.

But obviously I want to see the dream filled, fulfilled, out there and so far it hasn't happened.

Senator SCHATZ. Thank you.

Ms. Lippert, I have 2 questions for you.

The first, what's your mix of funding? I know, and could you separate out how much money actually flows through your Excelerator and then you, I think, you provided a number, 55 odd million in, I think, additional money raised, not necessarily coming through your organization.

Could you separate those out by dollar amount and also give us, it doesn't have to be precise, but a rough breakdown of Federal, State and private dollars?

Ms. LIPPERT. Yes, absolutely.

So on our funding side the rough breakdown of Federal, State and private funding is primarily Federal, very little State money and increasing private money.

So, on the Federal side primarily we've worked with the Office of Naval Research in the last couple of years. They have a commitment of $30 million over the next 5 years to fund this program which was seeded with Department of Energy money. So we really consider the Federal funding both Department of Energy and the Office of Naval Research funding as seed funding to prove out the vision.

I think there will always be a role for public funding in this kind of effort because we're trying to achieve some really broad public policy goals, but ultimately what we're trying to do is prove value there and use that to attract private funding. We attracted the first tranche of private funding on New Year's Eve, actually, of this year, so December 31st from Hawaiian Electric Industries. I think that's really the direction that we're going to make it a true public/private partnership.

On the company side we've invested approximately $10 million of Federal funding so far and the companies have turned that into $55 million of follow on funding.

Senator SCHATZ. Who owns the intellectual property?

Ms. LIPPERT. The companies. Yes.

So it's a traditional, sort of, Federal company relationship where the companies retain intellectual property, but the government has license to that intellectual property if it's of use to them.

So this is a highly leveraged program where we've been able to match make investors with the companies to directly put capital into the companies. But in the future what we see as our role is a more direct fund where we actually have relationships with these investors as well. But so far they've been directly investing into companies and into projects.

Senator SCHATZ. I'm just going to give you a minute to plug the why. That's my second question.

[Laughter.]

Ms. LIPPERT. OK, why unlimited renewable energy?

So, I mean, the question here is why do we have a group, maybe, promoting renewable energy?

Actually I think it goes back to something that we talked about yesterday at the ASCENT conference. It was one of the primary findings of our panel in public/private partnership which is the fundamental requirement for public/private partnership is trust. Why aren't—a way to help build trust in the community.

Then the second thing is just tapping into the diversity of our resources. I think it's just really about finding talent within our community and tapping into talent wherever that may be to help achieve a transformation that's real and tough, but really important.

Senator SCHATZ. Thank you very much.

My final question will be for Chairman Morita.

Could you just describe for the purposes of the record really, the Federal role in HCEI from the DOE and DOD perspective?

Ms. MORITA. OK, so first of all the partnership is extremely important to us. What it did was help bring resources to the State and help us leverage those resources in moving forward, accelerating the transformation to clean energy.

Currently, now, we are looking at how to update the agreement, the partnership between the State and DOE. It's been in effect since 2008 and the technologies have changed, priorities have changed. So looking forward to an updated agreement.

The other big issue is getting access to the national labs and the technical and economic expertise that they provide as we move forward. As I said in my testimony the technical and economic analyses will help us lead to better environmental and societal types of decisions. So just having that access to the expertise throughout the labs.

Then again, taking what we learned in Hawaii and having it applied to other areas. It, you know, we're outliers in this area and as Commissioner Akiba said, you know, we're a postcard from the future and so all eyes are on us right now as we move forward. I think in establishing partnerships, the systemic approach, that's what we can demonstrate and prove out for, not only the rest of the country, but the rest of the world.

Senator SCHATZ. Thank the panelists, thank you very much.

I want to thank the East-West Center. I want to thank the University of Hawaii Sea Grant and everybody in this room. We've had a very productive couple of days. I appreciate it very much.

[Whereupon, at 2:57 p.m. the hearing was adjourned.]

○